SUICIDE — THE LAST TABOO

A Professional Handbook in Search of Understanding

Preface by Richard Harries
Bishop of Oxford

Christopher Tadman-Robins

SUICIDE — THE LAST TABOO
A Professional Handbook in Search of Understanding

The Rhodes-Fulbright Library

by Christopher Tadman-Robins

ProdCode: CSS/250/272/4.57/28

Library of Congress
Catalog in Publication

2001087816

International Standard Book Number

1-55605-326-6

Printed in the United States of America

Wyndham Hall Press
Bristol, IN   46507-9460

Why do you pass judgement on your brother?
Or you, why do you despise your brother?
For we shall all stand before the judgement
seat of God; for it is written,
"As I live, says the Lord, every knee
shall bow to me,
and every tongue shall give praise to God."
So each of us shall give account of himself to God.

(Romans, 14: 10-12)

AUTHOR'S NOTE

Suicide is a very powerful and heart-rending issue that affects not only immediate family and friends, but church organisations and ultimately the whole community. Yet, thirty-five years on since the publication of 'Ought Suicide to be a Crime?', the Church of England remains remarkably silent about present statistics.

(Statistics drawn from the Samaritans Annual Review 2000: nearly 7,000 people in Great Britain take their lives every year, almost one suicide every 75 minutes, total 25% greater than annual road fatalities. An estimated 160,000 people attempt suicide every year. Young male suicide attempts have doubled in the last ten years, male suicides outnumber female suicides by 4:1).

In my view, the Church needs to re-examine this issue, not confining itself to questions of Christian conscience and bereavement, but rather how best to contribute more fully to a healing ministry to the despairing. It will need to consult a whole body of sociological and psychological research that explores not only social factors that cause society-induced stress (isolation, unemployment, financial and relationship difficulties) but also typical emotional impairment in childhood that renders some more vulnerable to despair in later life.

To be avoided also, is a tendency to rely exclusively on the Samaritans to minister to those at risk and the categorising of suicide merely as a 'medical problem', the result of chronic depression (rarely the sole motivating factor). Because 'poor copers' inside prison tend to consist of people who are also poor at coping in the community, there may be lessons to be learned from a pioneering 'prison branch' of the Samaritans, operating at present in Swansea Prison. Here, suicide and deliberate self-harm have been significantly reduced by facilitating an environment in which listening and talking is possible.

The recent 'Health of the Nation' documents aims to reduce overall suicide by 15% by the year 2000 (baseline 1990), challenging us to complement the work of other agencies in this field. However, resources of a pastoral nature are needed urgently, for in truth we are being called not only to a welfare revolution from without but a spiritual transformation from within. I call it a 'Theology of Living', a broad educative approach that embraces three basic objectives: the inculcation of knowledge about the incidence and characteristic of suicide; the influencing of attitudes to help eradicate stigma and the development of skills and strategies.

Clearly, suicide is not new, nevertheless, it remains a largely hidden phenomenon of the life experience of human society. Indeed, its 'hiddenness' has not only contributed towards its neglect as a cause for serious concern, but in church circles it long ago ceased to be a theme thought suitable for more explicit theological reflection.

If Christians fail to recognise self-inflicted death for what it is: the complete breakdown of life for the individual, we not only deny an important ministry to the helpless but we lose an opportunity to root the fundamental integrity of our belief in the hope of living.

C.T.-R.

TABLE OF CONTENTS

PREFACE

Most clergy and others engaged in pastoral ministry will be required, at some point, to deal first hand with cases of suicide or self-harm. At such times it is easy to feel out of one's depth as a pastor, or to be uncertain how to respond theologically to those who have taken, or wish to take, their own lives.

The care of those who may be suicidal or wish to harm themselves requires considerable expertise, often beyond the personal resources of a Christian minister. However, before professional help can be given warning signs need to be recognised, and support and guidance provided. This is often the point at which a minister can play a part.

Sadly, it is not always possible to spot the warning signs, and even when it is the help offered may not always prevent a tragedy from occurring. And so a further aspect of this ministry is to understand the probable causes of suicide and self-harm in order to help all concerned - including the minister — come to terms with what has happened.

Very little has been written to help the Christian minister deal with suicide and self-harm. This handbook is therefore a welcome addition to the literature. As well as providing practical advice grounded in research by psychologists and social scientists, it offers a much needed theological critique of suicide and self-harm.

This handbook is rooted in the personal experience of its author, and has developed from his work with the Oxford Diocesan Working Group on Suicide and Self Harm. Out of this working group the organisation SASH (Suicide And Self Harm) has been developed in the Oxford Diocese.

I warmly commend this handbook as a valuable contribution to the ministry of the Church.

Richard Harries
Bishop of Oxford

INTRODUCTION

From the Intercessions for Tuesday week 4 Morning Prayer of The Divine Office:

> Our sufferings bring acceptance, acceptance brings hope: and our hope will not deceive us, for the Spirit has been poured into our hearts. It is through the same Spirit that we pray: Stay with us Lord, on our journey.

Whenever I read this passage my mind is drawn to my most formative memory, the suicide of a close friend some thirty years ago. During the period that has elapsed I have known of a number of Christians who have died similarly. Most had accepted their sufferings though hope had eluded them. Others discovered a new kind of hope, a spirit that led them inexorably to the act, but, with an expectation of a greater life to come. In short, not 'journey's end' but 'to the faithful, death the gate of life' (John Milton, Paradise Lost).

This period of reflection culminated in 1992 with the suicide of my brother, a teacher and theologian, to whom this handbook is dedicated. Though his life always seemed curiously doomed, his was nonetheless, a largely productive life distinguished by a restless searching for that spirit that promises eternal life. We had on occasions, shared our ideas about life and death, and though it proved impossible to dissuade him from the fatal act, his demise has prompted a deeper exploration of not only the phenomenological and societal aspects but also the essentially Christian concerns relating to the reality of suffering.

Since then, I have initiated a Diocesan Working Group that is committed to the formation of a human resource to aid clergy and laity, who, unfamiliar with this territory, find themselves in need of advice, literature and appropriate referral when ministering to the hopeless and despairing person. This group (S.A.S.H.) (See relevant organisations – Appendix 4) continues to reflect, research and monitor developments in the understanding of suicide and self-harm and assists wherever possible in support of the bereaved.

I hope that this handbook will not only complement this work by drawing together the various factors involved in self-harm but also serve as a focus for those engaged in aiding outreach by the Church to helpless and depressed individuals tempted to suicide. It is my belief that, experience, exploration and reflection, logically precede authentic praxis and it is from this direct contact with victims and through a developing research body of knowledge, to which I have devoted much of my time as a minister, that this handbook has been brought to fruition

Laurie Green (1990:1) writes that the application of theology 'offers an exciting way of bringing together the crucial experiences of human living and the abiding truths of the Christian faith.' However, it is my belief that any exhaustive Christian responses to suicide and self harm should not operate in a 'theological vacuum'. In this enquiry, therefore, I have sought to draw upon not only Theological but also Sociological and Psychological disciplines so as to create an informed, comprehensive and accessible resource for use by clergy and laity.

This study, accordingly, falls into four main areas. In each chapter I have presented initially a body of information and insight, much of which can be followed up by further recommended reading if desired (see references) concluding with a final brief summary, in which I have pointed to areas of possible response and reflection.

Chapter One, examines two pressing concerns for Christians. Namely, how does faith respond to an act that denies fundamentally the value of life, and, can our knowledge of the motivation and morality that surrounds voluntary death enable us to better understand suicide as not only a feature of societal living, but also as a significant point of ministry. Since the predominant views of scripture are somewhat ambiguous, it was necessary to reflect upon those questions against a broad view of history that saw the censure of Augustine and Aquinas as decisive in forming Christian opinion.

Chapter Two, explores the collective and individual causes that are thought to contribute to suicidal crisis. In addition, on-going research into 'poor copers' in prison and in the community, helps reveal valuable insights into the appropriate application of a more sensitive and compassionate ministry of healing to the despairing.

Chapter Three, by investigating two contrasting case histories, seeks to identify important features of psychodynamic impairment associated with the family and the vulnerable individual to illustrate the characteristic pains and tensions of pastoral ministry to the suicidal. This prompts a call for the nurturing of imaginative strategies, within an education framework, to help combat the rising incidence of self-destructive harm amongst the young.

A final chapter concludes that a broad educative approach to the phenomenon of suicide is long overdue and that clergy and laity are better placed than we might imagine in helping reveal greater insight into the tragedy of self-harm. The hope is, that through the exercise and development of pastoral skills and strategies the Church can then play its part in influencing attitudes and eradicating stigma and ignorance.

CHAPTER ONE

SUICIDE - A QUESTION OF CHRISTIAN CONSCIENCE

The main thrust of this enquiry is my belief that (i) self-inflicted death, paradoxically, is an accepted part of the life-experience of human society; (ii) Christian responses to it can help reveal the theological integrity of its beliefs and provide for a significant point of ministry to both victim and the bereaved. Campbell and Collinson (1988: XVII) stress that the importance of suicide lies in the way it 'forces us to acknowledge that the ultimate choice - that of not existing - is always open to us and that in continuing to live we affirm, and are responsible for affirming, the value of life.' So, not surprisingly, suicide by denying the value of life threatens every one of us in a particularly fundamental way.

Therefore, to help Christians to understand this threat and to enable them to minister more effectively in its aftermath, careful attention needs to be given to the matter of a proper working definition of suicide, for this may well determine how the biblical evidence is to be identified and interpreted. Indeed, those who seek help from clergy and laity may well be asking questions about the morality of the act and also seeking to understand how they, the bereaved, ought to feel in the wake of such tragedy.

1. Formulating a Working Definition

Though we believe we understand suicide to be killing oneself, not all self-killings are suicide therefore intention is of paramount importance, some are vengeful and others may be symbolic (e.g. seppuku). Emile Durkhéim goes so far as to assert that all acts of self renunciation (e.g. the martyr dying for faith) are describable as suicide because 'at the moment of acting the victim knows the certain result of his conduct'. (Holland, 1969:73 and Durkhéim, [1897] 1951:44)

Similarly, Andersberg (1989: 56) argues that inclusiveness is of crucial importance, so that it may be said a person instigates:

> .... a course of events, of which he is an active or passive participant, where the greater majority, of his simple actions (or non-constituents) are performed with the intention to shorten life, for whatever motive, good or

> bad, and for which death follows in the way he had
> planned, or a least in a way he could accept.

This definition assumes that it is possible to truly **know** what the individual wanted and fully comprehended in his actions.

However, Edwin Schneidman (1976:5) argues that, in fact, no one really knows why human beings commit suicide, 'indeed the very person who takes his own life may be least aware at the moment of decision the essence (much less the totality) of his reasons and emotions for doing so,' so, not unnaturally, his definition has a medical ring to it:

> ...a conscious act of self-induced annihilation, best understood
> as a multi-dimensional malaise in a needful individual who defines
> an issue for which the suicide is perceived as the best solution.
> (1985:17)

This definition is very technical and it does not, for the purpose of this enquiry, address the essential religious and theological concerns though it is free of any valued judgements, a special concern of Harry Kuitert (1985:103). What is required of this study, is a definition that describes simply the deliberate ending of life whatever the conditions, intentions or means to achieve it.

Niceto Blazequéz (Kuitert, 1985:63) comes closest to this ideal with the following: 'Suicide is the act by which a person directly, knowingly and freely brings about his own death' (regardless of motives, circumstances or method). This, I believe, adequately addresses the essentials of freedom of choice and consciousness of action whilst leaving open the reasons or intentions behind the act.

Using this definition as our starting point we can now begin to examine biblical evidence with an eye to a broad range of issues. For example, is suicide always and in itself wrong; can such wrongness be mitigated by certain conditions; does the Bible condemn or condone conclusively voluntary death, or, does the act receive its moral colouring from the integrity of the characters and their purposes in committing it? Any Christian response will need to address those types of question sensitively, bearing in mind that though suicide may not necessarily be the worst of sins, like murder, it is by virtue of its finality arguably the most destructive.

2. What can the Bible tell us?

Of major importance to the unsuccessful suicide and the bereaved is the primary question why? Why am I still alive, or why did he do it? But for a Christian there is often the compelling question why do I feel such a loathing and guilt at what has happened, and, how can the Christian faith help me to understand it? It is at this point of great personal need that applying theology can be crucial, for suicide is rarely discussed openly and critically in Church circles. I will argue that without the traditional benefits of preaching, discussion and reflection both laity and clergy may be at a serious disadvantage in addressing an issue that challenges everyone. Therefore, any opportunity to address this issue by way of discussion or house group will benefit local pastoral outreach.

Of equal importance, the Church at large will run the risk of contributing to its own appearance of irrelevance if applied theology is not mobilised to confront the biblical evidence before attempting to formulate an effective Christian response. Blazequéz' definition will, I believe, adequately embrace not only the despairing and remorseful suicide (Judas) the voluntary death that today resembles active euthanasia (King Saul) but even, the willing self-sacrifice of Jesus himself. For his death, together with those of the early Christian martyrs might be categorised as the result of indirect and altruistic suicide.

Though the Hebrew Scriptures and the New Testament provides a variety of recorded suicides, it is of paramount importance that the reader remains objective in considering how the act was recorded and for what purpose. Also, in addressing the question of whether the Bible condemns or condones suicide, the inherent danger of reading into the text one's previously-held views (eisegesis) is well recognised as a way of misusing the evidence to argue one way or the other.

(a) Old Testament

Not surprisingly, the Old Testament suicides are all men of nobility beginning with Saul, who, following a hideous battle in which three of his sons are killed, faces captivity and torture. He demands that his armour bearer should despatch him but at his refusal Saul falls upon his sword, as does his servant. (1Sam. 1-13 31: 4-8). In the aftermath his body is reclaimed and treated with great respect. Even in the alternative account (2Sam.1:1-16) in which a young Amalakite claims to have killed Saul at his request, there is no evidence of stigma. Indeed David offers a poignant lament on his death (2Sam. 1:24-25a) with those who buried and honoured Saul receiving blessings. (2Sam. 2:46-7).

Similarly, the authors do not condemn the suicides of Ahith'opel, trusted advisor to would-be king Absalom who hangs himself after his counsel is rejected (2 Sam. 17:23) and Zimri who set fire to his house in a city under siege (1 Kings. 16: 18-19). No stigma or penalty is recorded and, though Zimri is condemned for his sins, the manner of his death is not criticised.

Sampson's spectacular death in demolishing the house about him, and by so doing punishing his enemies (Judges. 16:28-31) also attracts respect, his name included in the Epistle to the Hebrews (11:32) as a remembered hero. Similarly, Abimelech's death (Judges 9: 52-54) following his fatal wounding by a woman is recorded as an honourable one, for he commands his servant to run him through.

Jonah's moment of peril (Jon. 1-4) though not usually considered an attempted suicide, does meet Blazequéz' definition and with it introduces a Durkhéimian dimension of social altruism, the men complying with his request to be thrown overboard. By so doing, the author appears to suggest that his attempted suicide is even God inspired.

(b) New Testament

It is when we come to the New Testament that our perspective widens for we are no longer solely concerned with whether authors see voluntary death as reprehensible but rather are there any significant questions of mitigation to be addressed i.e. motive and circumstance. In the case of Judas, for example, was it love of money, resentment at being excluded from the inner circle of Peter, James and John or irritation at Jesus' apparent failure which lead to his bitterness and disillusion? For though his treachery appears shameful it is no more than Peter's who denies Christ, or those disciples who left Jesus and fled from Gethsemane.

There are two accounts of how Judas died at his own hand in Matthew 27: 3-5 by hanging and in Acts 1:18 as the result of a fall. In the former it appears that the author's implicit judgement is that he is condemned for betraying his master, but not for killing himself. This presumably comes about as the result of remorse and repentance, so Judas' self-killing receives no censure the act already regarded perhaps as acceptable in certain conditions.

An attempted suicide that, unlike Jonah's, is thwarted by a human and not by God, is the case of the Philippean jailer (Acts 16: 19-34) who thinking he has allowed his prisoners to escape, draws his sword to kill himself. Paul reassures him and he does not accomplish the act, but, this incident does raise the question for what purpose does the author tell the story? Perhaps it was intended to illustrate that Paul has a high regard for human life and in recognising the jailer's sense of honour, he receives no outright condemnation.

(c) Jesus an 'Indirect suicide'?

We cannot examine the New Testament without noting a central Christian belief that Jesus himself chose to die on a cross in order to bring salvation to the world. If in his choosing, albeit for the highest of motives, his death can be construed as suicide, then might his act conceivably be of some very real comfort to those who recognise voluntary death in certain circumstances to be acceptable, or at the very least, permitted?

For it can be argued that, using the principles of deontic logic (logic of norms, a contribution that Kant makes to this debate) this action is neither commended nor apparently forbidden. In which case it may be possible to advance a proposition that freedom (i.e. moral freedom that is always related to the freedom of others) not life, is the ultimate human good. Because it is not the fact that man is alive that makes him human, for though life is necessary it is not a sufficient condition for being human. What is sufficient for man to exist as man i.e. in accordance with human dignity, is freedom. Only as a free living being is man completely human and the realisation of that freedom may involve the possibility of suicide under exceptional circumstances.

Whatever we believe Jesus to be, he was clearly human, so exploring any claim that Jesus commits suicide it will be important to look at the question of his non-resistance to a train of events which led to his death. *The New Encyclopaedia* (Kane, 1967: 781-83) tries to clarify this question by distinguishing between 'direct suicide', when one has the intention of causing one's own death as a thing desired for its own sake or as a means to an end, and 'indirect suicide', when death itself is not desired but simply seen as a consequence of an act, even of non-resistance. (Both Tertullian and Origen describe Jesus' death as a voluntary one).

Though Jesus' death might be best described as an 'indirect suicide' i.e. his non-resistance 'freely bring about his own death' so meeting our working definition, the integrity of the act will depend, nevertheless, on how we see the essential figure of Jesus and the motives prevailing.

First, there is the man who prays 'let this cup pass from me: nevertheless your will be done' (Matt. 26:39) who is reluctant to die yet ready to suffer. Second, there is the divine side, where he surrenders to death as part of a cosmic plan, the Son of God's 'hour of glory'. The outcome is somewhat ambiguous, for though human choice in Jesus' case is fundamental, it may not be of prime importance as the ultimate motivating factor, which is why, presumably, the early Christians interpret his death as the archetypal atoning sacrifice of a righteous person that saves all people. (1.Cor.15: 3-5)

However, it is worth noting that Jesus appears to have had a number of opportunities to die at the hands of others, notably as reported in Luke's Gospel (4:29-30) where his decision to go to Jerusalem seems to be a response to a deep conviction that what must be, must be (9:51). Similarly, in John's Gospel the writer appears to conclude that Jesus actively avoids capture and stoning (8:59, 10:31, 7:30 and 8:20) and by emphasising this he points to a perceived response of Jesus to the providential timing of his Father. Even in his non-resistance he therefore seems to be in control (18:4-7) refusing to defend himself (19:1) preparing to surrender to a certain death.

By exhorting his followers to do likewise, as Mark reports it (8:34-35) he influences not only those who take up their cross, but also inspires Paul in his own agonising decision to live or die: 'For to me to live is Christ, and to die is gain'. (Phil. 1:21-26) In those words we can sense that life for Paul is a struggle: imprisoned (Phil. 1:7, 13, 14, 17) afflicted (1:17; 4:14) he suffers willingly for Christ (3:10, 1:30, 2:27) suffering deprivation and hunger. (4:11-12) In short, he conformed to the death of Christ (3:10; 2:17) in a sense dying daily (1Cor. 15:31) accepting beatings, prison and even shipwreck (2Cor. 5:1-18; 6:4-5; 11:24-29)

(d) Paul a 'Potential Suicide'?

In purely historical terms there seems to have been a widespread acceptance of voluntary death among Paul's contemporaries. However, his discussion here is more about responding to the command to witness whatever the cost than merely provoking martyrdom. So, like Socrates' view in Plato's *Phaedo*, that an individual is forbidden to kill himself until God brings some necessity or demand upon him (anangke) so Paul, though considering voluntary death finally rejects it because it runs contrary to what he believes is the present will of God.

The additional question of the ownership of one's body is also significant, the Cynics had always maintained the right and freedom to take their own lives. But Paul appears to contradict this by his assertion that believers belong to God (1Cor. 6:19-20) so, like Ambrose[1] he believes that the Christian ought to stay at his post until God gives the command.

If 'to live is Christ, and to die is gain' then presumably to embrace death like Christ i.e. accepting under certain circumstances that for the glory of God there is no other way, is to sanction 'indirect suicide'. As we shall see later, John Donne in *Biathanatos* comments on this famous letter of Paul's to the Phillipians arguing that although suicide in most cases is sinful i.e. a deed and desire contrary to the eternal law of God, in certain distinct cases it is not. For suicide is not inherently sinful, its moral status depends on what and how the act has been inspired and the specific circumstances surrounding it. (Donne, [1744] 1984:58).

In brief, the New Testament reveals no specific condemnation of voluntary death, but it might be said that the authors of the gospels have created a model: Jesus, who dies by his own choice, voluntarily, but in accordance with God's plan, so that raised from the dead he may be exalted to heaven promising the same for those who follow him. Not surprisingly, given the period, many took him at his word and re-enactment of his death was taken quite literally.

3. Some Theological and Philosophical Insights

It appears that scriptural accounts of suicide are told without a clear intention of condemning the act, the focus being rather on how individuals have lived not how they chose to die. Lloyd R. Bailey (Clemons, 1990:100) writes that 'perhaps the most that can be said is that the issue... is an ambiguous one, and the Bible is an accurate reflection of that ambiguity'. If this is so, then it might be prudent, when exploring the rather diffuse truths of scripture, to identify views that at least predominate, and from them, attempt to shape appropriate Christian responses to the issue.

(a) Suicide - an issue of ambiguity

Today, the most common condemnation of suicide is grounded in the belief that this deliberate act violates God's creation i.e. Life is a gift and therefore God alone has the power to take it back. Genesis (Gen. 1:1-2; 4a, 2;2;4b-25) affirms that God is the ultimate force of life as does 1 Sam. 2:6 and the opening verses of John's Gospel. Also, that Christ's coming enables us to have life 'more abundantly' (10:10) which may imply that death by choice is contrary to God's intent.

We are aware of the same in the predicament of Job, because the fundamental reason for his phenomenal endurance in spite of extreme human misery is his belief that (like Ps. 104: 27-30 and Eccl. 3:1-3) only the Lord gave and only the Lord is to take away. (Job. 1:20-21) Thomas Aquinas pursues the same argument using deuteronomic texts (32-39) which speak of a God who solely kills and makes alive.

In addition, the notion of God-given wisdom as a basis for life is not uncommon in the Old Testament and with it the assumption that failure to accept it is to reject God's wishes, i.e. to love death is to go against God. However, a prevalent Christian belief is that such wisdom is distinguished by a freedom to make mistakes and to receive forgiveness and that where there is failure nothing separates humankind from the love of God. (Rom. 8:38).

A specific prohibition that might be applied to encompass self-destruction is the sixth commandment: 'You shall not kill' (Ex. 20:13; Deut. 5:17). As we shall see both Augustine and Aquinas quote this injunction extensively and yet there are problems, because most scholars today believe that the contextual thinking behind this Hebrew word: 'quatal' to kill or murder, was primarily to prevent the Israelites from taking the law into their own hand. Clearly, not all killing is murder, so why is suicide necessarily considered self-murder? Even Augustine concedes exceptions to voluntary death, such as a result of rape or unavoidable martyrdom.

From the same book (Deut. 4:9) Israelites are urged to 'keep your soul diligently', and so like Aristotle (1926: Book V 1138a 9-13) to deny others your contribution to society by voluntary death, is not to 'choose life' (Deut. 30:19; Ex.18:13-32). Yet, the doctrine that human society has a prior claim to the life of the individual has never been an obstacle to the person considering suicide, all too often consideration of relatives and friends has not restrained the person who in that terrible isolation contemplates self-destruction. It falls to Christ to demonstrate that God alone has a prior call on an individual's loyalty.

Both Matthew (10:28) and Luke (12:4-5) go further in emphasising that one ought to fear God, who alone is capable of destroying both body and soul. In any event your body is not your own says Paul (1Cor. 6:19-20) so take good care of it, do not abuse it[2]. Hence in Ephesians 5:29 he is very persuasive in urging all to love others as you would love yourself. Like Job, Christians are bidden to endure and to suffer persecution if necessary (1Pet.1:6-9) and above all to hold on to life, this being in itself, an expression of faith. Such sentiments are similar to the basic philosophy of the Greeks, especially the Stoics which influenced strongly Christian ethics. Later, Augustine (1972:117) writes: 'the truly noble soul will bear all suffering', however, the numbers must be legion of those who did indeed suffer but finally could bear no longer an intolerable life.

Much of the conflict in these arguments, I would suggest, hinges on the question of maintaining some sort of balance about the significance given to earthly life in the whole cosmic scheme. 'Indirect suicide' can include the giving willingly of one's live in the midst of persecution as the ultimate expression of faithfulness. Yet, as we shall see, much of the foundation on which the established church based its beliefs is thanks to Augustine's rejection of this. Indeed, in the New Testament followers were inspired by the testimony to take up their cross (Mk. 8:35-35; Matt.10:30; Luke 9:24; 14:26-27; 17:33 and John 12:25) Mark's words (10:42-45) speaking of Jesus who 'gives his life as a ransom for many.'

There is, of course, a danger that in identifying texts that speak graphically of sacrifice for others, (John 15:12-24) some may use scripture not only to favour 'indirect suicide' but to offer a blanket condoning of voluntary death in all circumstances. This is to be resisted because it seems clear that such deaths were evaluated in different ways in antiquity. However, the idea that killing oneself was both a sin and a crime is a relatively late Christian development, its impetus derived from Augustine's polemics against the self-destructive mania of the Donatists (late fourth century). Before this the act had been respected, admired and sought after as a means of attaining immortality. It was ironic, therefore, that later theologians should condemn it as a sin for which Christ's similar act could not atone.

Writers on Philosophy such as Camus (1955) Dodds (1965:135) and Nock (1933:197) attest to the prevalence of a 'suicide cult' in Greek literature as early as Homer. Both Plato and Aristotle concede man's need to commit suicide where there is devastating misfortune and intolerable shame. The Cynics offer this alternative so as to 'live according to nature' whilst the Epicureans saw freedom from fear, that might be relieved by a welcome death, as the ultimate goal of life.

Around 300BC the Hellenistic period saw strikingly different responses to the fundamental problem of death in Jewish circles. Apocalyptic eschatology caused the finality of death to be seen more as a resurrection experience. So that later portions of the Hebrew Bible provided further evidence of a vindication for the righteous who chose death. (Second Isaiah 40-55; Ps. 44:9-12; Jer.11:18-20; Isa.53:10-12). The suffering servant texts point to a new age to come where death is no longer seen as an exit from life but a step towards salvation.

It is important to realise that these beliefs take their truth from a notion of voluntary death related to a basic dualistic understanding of the universe - of a material world against spiritual experience. Josephus, self-styled apologist for the Jewish people makes much reference to voluntary death in his *Jewish Antiquities* praising the acts of courage of the Maccabean revolt and the mass suicide in Masada. He, like Philo, draws on Rabbinic material (*Mishnah, Talmud and Midrash*) that speaks of choosing death over humiliation and torture to gain eternal life. Indeed, it is only a relatively late post-Talmudic tractate (*Semahot*) that specific laws are formulated regarding suicide, most of which are concerned to establish intent.

Before we look next at the arguments and context surrounding Augustine's responses to what he considered reckless martyrdom, (a thesis that was decisive in forming Christian opinion) it may be worth reflecting that attitudes to direct or indirect suicide have always been subject to the influence of changes historically in the development of society.

(b) Martyrdom - Augustine's argument

We shall see, beginning with the martyrdom of Stephen (Acts.7:54-60) about 40AD that as Christianity expanded, so the pre-occupation with death continued. Ignatius of Antioch, condemned to death in 107AD, writes to Churches in Asia Minor, pleading that no effort should be made to save him. His attitude, like Origen, is typical of a form of martyrdom that was believed to bring with it special privileges. In 197AD Tertullian writes 'Nothing matters to us in this age, but to escape from it with all speed' (*Apology* 41.5) life was seen at best as unimportant; at worst, evil (Alvarez 1971:68).

Nevertheless, there were important voices that criticised these theatrical displays and it was seen as crucial that for these acts to be deemed authentic, there should be genuine evidence of a response to a divine signal, though no one describes precisely what this might be. The central problem (Letters of Pliny) seems to have been one of allegiance, Christians simply refusing to acknowledge the Roman Emperor as God provoking terrible slaughter (Melmoth and Hutchinson, 1924).

It is against this historical background that Augustine's work is set in which he protests that deliberately seeking death is not the best way to demonstrate faith, and so (with a few exceptions) it is seen as a grave sin. His argument is without precedent in appealing to the Six Commandment and his teaching became the official stance of the Church from about 450AD to the present day.

In the early chapter of *The City of God* (Book 1. Section 20) the Sixth Commandment is used to argue that it prohibits both the killing of another and yourself, yet there is no evidence from any Jewish or Christian writer before him that this forbids suicide. He allows killing in war, capital punishment and in Sampson's case he argues that there must have been divine inspiration. In addition, he allows further exceptions for virgins and married women who are raped or threatened with sexual abuse in times of persecution. Indeed, there are numerous accounts of women taking their lives in these circumstances, some of whom are venerated in the Catholic Church as Saints and Martyrs inspite of their self-inflicted deaths.

Here, Augustine appears to have been heavily influenced by Bishop Ambrose, who converted and baptised him into Christianity in 387AD. Ten years previously Ambrose wrote a treatise *Concerning Virgins* (Ambrose, 1896) that dealt with this question, broadly providing for the exceptions as above. But, one must ask, where is the evidence for 'secret instructions' or supernatural divine signals that are meant to excuse such suicides?

In the *New Catholic Encyclopaedia* (1967: XIII 782) the author comments. 'If suicide is intrinsically evil, God could not command it, and it is not true... that direct suicide is permissible if it is committed in response to a special inspiration of God, the Lord of Life and Death.'   Yet the Church's censure of suicide is based on a foundation of tradition that finds its roots in Augustine. Either the earliest martyrs are saints and therefore there is an exception, or they are not.

A clue to the driving force behind Augustine's view is perhaps the belief that he was, in truth, reacting against a prevalent Stoic philosophy that man's essential nature is defined by his being a rational animal, in which case a willingness to take one's own life may be seen as a real test of one's indifference to death.

Freud, in this century, spoke of the 'death instinct' as the negative side of the unsatiated drives of the libido, so Seneca spoke of the 'libido moriendi' describing how a slavish following of the pleasure principle leads to a disgust in oneself and life. However, we are mistaken if we believe the Stoic recommendation of suicide is directed to those who are beaten by life, rather it is to those who have mastered life: 'suicide as an escape, dictated by fear, contradicts the stoic courage to be.' (Tillick, 1952:12)

For the Stoic, suicide was a means of affirming rationality and one's essential humanity in the face of dehumanising circumstances, and, by so doing exercising also, freedom from and indifference to the lower feelings and appetites of living. However, Augustine attacks Stoic, moral rigorism as merely a form of suppression, which in time may encourage an attitude of resigned despair.

(c) A Mortal Sin - Aquinas' Statement

While it was Augustine who first linked the sixth Commandment with the prohibition against suicide, it was Thomas Aquinas who developed the theological statement in his *Summa Theologica*, which combined traditional teachings of the Church with the ideas of Aristotle.   In his treatise (2.2.65.5) Aquinas provides three reasons for why suicide ought to be considered a mortal sin (a) because it is a denial of self-love, (b) because it is a rejection of obligation to others, and (c) because life is a God-given gift.

He sees suicide as not only contrary to 'natural law', the instinctive human desire to preserve and cherish life, but also Christian belief. Indeed, the text taken from Matthew 19:19 'love your neighbour as yourself' (Lev. 19:18) simply does not make sense to people for whom the idea of death is **not** something to be avoided.   What Christ says is rather, love your neighbour in the way you would love yourself. Today, people who feel tempted to suicide often demonstrate great personal inadequacy revealed in depression and personality problems (as in my brother's case destroying themselves when their sense of love for themselves and for life becomes meaningless) labelling this as 'mortal sin' is not, I believe, a way forward.

Aquinas argues that no person is a judge of himself, his judgement is submitted to God's therefore his fate is not for him to decide, he is merely adopting a greater evil to escape a less. However, clearly Christians too can resort to suicide when the pain of living is intolerable, so perhaps suicide may be viewed not so much as sin but as the direct result of a pervasive lack of an appropriate self-love.

Although Aquinas' reason that suicide 'injures the community' is based on the philosophy of Aristotle, where the state would be deprived of a citizen and a tax payer, it does contain an element of truth. The effects on the morale of family, friends and community is undeniable, whilst the loss of potential development of the individual and their contribution to society is enormous. His final reason, that life is God's gift (Gen. 2:7) is based on the notion that man's free-will is subject still to the power of God.

(d) The Challenge of Individualism

Though paradoxically the Middle Ages displayed an intense preoccupation with death in all its most horrifying details, the taboo against suicide nevertheless remained intact until the late Renaissance. What followed was an insistence on a form of individualism which saw its right to challenge Christian beliefs and morals. Voltaire, Hume and Schopenhauer were in the forefront but the most remarkable was John Donne, priest, poet and writer, who in 1608 wrote *Biathanatos - A Declaration of that Paradox, or Thesis, that self-homicide is not so naturally sinne, that it may never be otherwise.*

Constantly tempted by suicide he justifies it, though he agrees that it is neither rational nor dignified, people kill themselves in reality because life has become intolerable for them. In relation to the theories of Augustine and Aquinas he examines the concept of 'natural law'. Quoting Paul (Rom2:14-15) he describes the Gentiles as 'doing by nature what law requires', if this is true he says everything we do which does not concur precisely with our religion will be a 'sin against nature'. However, there is nothing in the law that prohibits suicide.

The Age of Reason which followed gave suicide a life of its own as an extra-literary topic with writers such a William Cowper and Thomas Chatterton. The taboo was gradually being removed whilst the great romantic writers and poets (Wordsworth, Coleridge, Keats, Shelley and Byron) were positively inspired by self-death as an end in itself. Thus how you die no longer decides how eternity is to be spent, it merely sums up your life: 'if suicide is allowed then everything is allowed.' (Wittgenstein, 1961:91)

At this point we ought to make mention that the defence of suicide on the grounds of man's rational nature, which finds its source in the Stoic philosophy of Seneca and Marcus Aurelius, is argued similarly by Kant but on strictly logical terms. His maxim is 'From self-love I make it my principle to shorten my life, if its continuance threatens more evil than it promises pleasure....' (Kant 1948:53-54) He believes that the suicide must ask himself whether it is rational for such an action to become a universal law of nature. His conclusion is that suicide is indeed irrational, that there are no justifiable reasons for it, only causes which are seen as pathological disturbances.

Much later, Nietzsche advocates the celebration of self death as 'ecstatic fulfilment', 'My death I commend unto you, free death, that cometh unto me because I will.' (Nietzsche, 1958:37) Even Bonhoeffer is moved to similar sentiments, that death is either the consummating end of life or a celebration of hope of eternal life: 'freedom, long have we sought thee in discipline and in action and in suffering. Dying, we behold thee now, and see thee in the face of God'. (Bonhoeffer, 1959:161-2)

Before long, individualism has already begun to give to suicide the character of liberty and spontaneity that was, in some ways, reminiscent of the early church but for strictly personal reasons of fulfilment and independence. There followed a renewed study of suicide as a primarily social phenomenon to which Durkhéim's classic, *Suicide: A Study in Sociology* ([1897] 1952) points no longer to the morality of the act but the social conditions which can produce such despair.   No longer seen as irredeemable moral crime, but as a fact of society, fuelled by social causes, suicide is treated as a phenomenon to be discussed and analysed.

4. Summary

It seems apparent that once we have determined for ourselves what suicide is said to be: 'an act by which a person directly, knowingly and freely brings about his own death,' then Christians today will want to concern themselves not simply with the morality of the action but the context and motivation that surrounds it, therein lays a challenging opportunity to minister.

The Bible whilst it neither explicitly condemns or condones voluntary death, it does, at least by implication, assume that life is given to be cherished. But, by the time of Augustine censure had increased if only for utilitarian reasons, too many were sacrificing their lives for their faith, and therefore convincing reasons has to be found to staunch the haemorrhage of suicide.

Undoubtedly a major contributory factor was Jesus' own act of choosing to die on the cross, the result of conscious non-violent resistance to aggression. The ambiguity of the act was sufficient to encourage others to emulate him. In addition, Paul's writings, though not sanctioning such sacrifice directly, served to support overt witness to faith whatever the cost.

Today the most common condemnation of suicide centres on the act as a violation of God's creation. However, where life has become intolerable and therefore meaningless some today might be tempted to put freedom at a higher value than life itself.

This belief is that though the fact that humankind are alive makes us human, it is not of itself sufficient condition for being human. Rather, it is that only in accordance with human dignity, does human kind desire to be free-living beings, i.e. completely human. Both Barth in the Ethics section of his *Church Dogmatics* (III/4) and Bonhoeffer ([1947] 1971) explore the basis of such a response in their writings, where the notion of freedom is never treated as an absolute but is always subject to qualification.

Even so, for the Christian, the exercise of freedom will always mean in relation to the wishes of the author of life, clearly we do not **own** life. Both Barth and Bonhoeffer are in agreement that human kind is free to possess life or destroy it, but this does not endow a **right** to life except for a definite service. Similarly, humankind has a **right** to death, but only in obedience to God's wishes (John 10:17) both accrue from the free giving of life.

Both Augustine and Aquinas also quote the sixth commandment to aid their argument, however, not all killing is murder so why assume that suicide should necessarily be considered similarly. By offering exceptions Augustine's thesis is further undermined.

In reality, the power, I believe, to tolerate a painful life for some, can only come from a belief that it is part of an expression of faith, whatever the cost. But, only small proportions of human kind have such a degree of faith so are the others to be condemned for lack of it? Such a blanket disapproval of voluntary death is, I believe, out of place today.

Finally, Aquinas' statement that suicide should be considered a mortal sin because it is a denial of self-love is, I feel, open to further exploration than merely on the basis of 'natural law'. The way in which individuals perceive and accept themselves will no doubt affect the way they treat themselves and others. He argues that no person is a judge of himself, but this statement needs to be balanced against the freedom given to human kind to make what they can of life and their place in it. Perhaps as John Donne puts it, people kill themselves not out of defiance or recklessness so much as out of crippling despair. There is a level of suffering (that varies from person to person) that no human being is able to tolerate, even on the pain of eternal damnation.

In conclusion, scripture adequately illustrates the ongoing tragedy of suicide in history, the Good News offering to the despairing repentance and mercy and calling all Christians to help shoulder the burden by way of comfort and compassion. It is important to realise, however, that 'a man who can no longer live is not helped by any command that he should, but only by a new spirit'. (Bonhoeffer, 1955:125) Nevertheless, it is a voice that some desperate people cannot hear or will not listen to and so their deaths remain a tragedy.

It is my belief that by giving this issue a greater priority and by considering suicide not only in terms of an offence against God, but as a societal problem of breakdown, in which there is a degree of impaired psychodynamic development, Christians might be better equipped to assess risk and crucially respond to this trauma as a significant part of ministry.

§ § §

ENDNOTES

1. On Phil. 1:21 Ambrose writes in *Oh death as a God,* likening man's loyalty to the Emperor to that of witnessing to Christ as King: 'Do they abandon their posts without the Emperor's consent? Yet what a greater thing it is to please the divine than the human'. (Droge, A. J. and Tabor, J. D. 1992:124)

2. Plato is aware of this issue also, his view is that there are claims by the Gods and state over individual rights. Paul's position is borne out by Ambrose in the fourth century AD in his homiletical treatise: *On Death as a good*, he offers the following exposition of Phil.1:21 (Droge and Tabor, 1922:124) Thus for the saint 'to live is Christ and to die is gain'. He does not flee the servitude of life like a slave, and yet like a wise man he does embrace the gain of death.

CHAPTER TWO

SUICIDE -A QUESTION OF SOCIOLOGICAL INFLUENCES

1. Durkhéim and the Significance of Social Bonds

Chapter 1 has been concerned with suicide as a phenomenon that challenged Christian belief. In short, the Church was concerned with the validity of such an action before God, i.e. as a question of Christian conscience. However, with the upsurge of individualism in the seventeenth century, suicide was beginning to be seen as not just an issue of sin. There was a growing belief that other factors would need to be considered in any explanation of suicide as a phenomenon of human society. Modern, post-enlightenment times now began to see suicide more as a condition that afflicted a victim caused by factors in the environment. Scientific investigation of the 'internal' environment became the domain of medico-psychiatric enquiry (See Chapter 3) while with the advent of national vital statistics in the early nineteenth century, studies of the effects of the 'external environment' on the collective phenomenon became the province of the sociologist.

Nevertheless, the earliest sociologists were the so-called 'moral statisticians' such as Quetelet, Guerry, Wagner and Morselli, who regarded statistics on suicide, as precise indicators of the state of society, seeing in their increase a moral crisis for Western Civilisation. Such enquiries sought to establish empirical correlations between suicide rate and major social factors.

(a) Suicide Rates

Durkhéim ([1987] 1952:152) drew heavily upon the same sources in formulating a typology of suicide in which categories of suicides were seen as products of specific social situations. His thesis was that there is an essential distinction between the explanations of variations in suicide rates and the aetiology of any given case. By statistical examination he explained that regularities in the social distribution of the suicide rate (SR) could show the following:

(i)   The SR varies with a state's established religion i.e. the greater the proportion of Protestants (more liberal and individual not so subject to the influences of a more authoritarian teaching typical of Catholicism) the higher SR.
(ii) The SR varies indirectly with family size, the larger the family the lower the SR.
(iii) The SR varies with political and national crises (lower during wartime and election campaigns).
(iv) The SR varies with a state's economic condition (higher during periods of economic success or crisis - 'boom or bust').
(v)   The SR varied with the particular occupational group (in the nineteenth century the industrial and commercial sphere had a higher SR than in the agricultural world).
(vi) The SR varies directly with a state's rate of divorce, the higher the rate the higher the SR.

At its simplest Durkhéim's theory asserts the single proposition that the state of 'social bonds' are the means by which individuals and society are connected.   This finding alone is of great relevance to any Christian responses, for the weaknesses of such bonds may be ameliorated by the active promotion of a more cohesive and unified society.

(b) Integrative and Regulative Bonds

Such bonds are moral in nature and can be sub-divided into two types:

(i)   Integrative bonds - which refer to the individual's attachment to the norms, beliefs and values of society.
(ii) Regulative Bonds - which refer to the means by which society holds in check individual desires and appetites.

Durkhéim maintained that a society in equilibrium will have the appropriate degree of integration and regulation and its suicide rate will be normal for its type. However, where the amount of integration or regulation varies from the equilibrium levels then societal dis-equilibrium results. Durkhéim identifies four logical possibilities:
Inadequate Integration (Egoistic Suicide) where the individual remains separate and alone from society, utilising solely their own resources.

Excessive Integration (Altruistic Suicide) where the individual is prepared to die for another or a principle, promoted by an excessive desire for self-sacrifice.

Inadequate Regulation (Anomic Suicide) where the individual suffers as a result of major changes in social position.

Excessive Regulation (Fatalistic Suicide) where the individual's future is blocked, choked by oppressive discipline (e.g. a totalitarian state).

In each case there will be a SR, it is the balance between each, Durkhéim emphasises that creates an SR normal for its type of society. Thus regularities such as established religion and family can express conditions of both inadequate integration and regulation. He concluded that religion could produce a preventative effect on suicide not primarily because of religious condemnation (the Catholic view) but because it was a society in which a number of beliefs and practices were favourable to a cohesive lifestyle shared in common - 'intense cohesive life' (1971:70). Nevertheless, Protestantism was still considered as less prophylactic of suicide because of the increased potential for secular influences, a factor in the increased disintegration of the ties of the individual to the group.

(c) Anomic and Egoistic Suicide

The nineteenth century witnessed not only changes consequent upon earlier religions, political and domestic 'revelations' but most of all the effects of the industrial revolution. Here, Anomic Suicide (inadequate regulation) highlighted that sense of 'loss of place' or the experience of 'not knowing one's place' that flows from sudden changes of fortune.

Since one's sense of social status, where one belongs, and what one may reasonably aspire to are largely given by one's occupational rank in society, any disruption of these supports to the individual weakened and precarious through poor upbringing, is potentially very serious. Whether the crisis is 'boom or bust', the effect is to upset the balance of social living. An example of this may be seen in the financial strictures and unemployment of the 1990's following the boom of the 1970's and '80's. (See Figure 1).

FIGURE 1

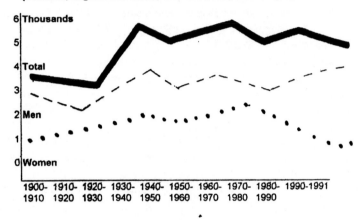

Suicide among men and women

(Scotland, England and Wales, 1900-1991, ten year averages)

Samaritans, 1993

Today, suicides by men, usually the primary 'bread winners' now outnumber women by a ratio of 4:1 with the fastest growing suicide rate in the under 25 age group. Simon Armson, the Samaritan's Chief Executive has commented: "It seems the pressure of living in the nineties combined with a reluctance to talk about feelings can be too much to cope with." (Samaritan News Autumn 1992)

It appears then, that social change can bring about startling moral de-regulation of which easy divorce is a good example. Similarly, unmarried people show higher rates of suicide than married people of the same age group, the SR decreasing in proportion to increasing family size. Suicide is hence said to vary inversely with the degree of integration of the social groups of which the individual forms a part. (Durkhéim, 1952:209).

This is particularly relevant when we examine the 'collective tenden-cies' of the Church. In the West, those countries which are predominantly Catholic have lower rates of suicide, in general, than those which are chiefly Protestant. Since both condemned suicide Durkhéim concludes that the reasons are to be found in the social fabric of each (see Table 1). Contrasting the Catholic Church with its well-established and closely woven set of beliefs, with the Protestant Church, more individualised and committed to the 'Spirit of free enquiry that animates this religion' (1952: 158) he believes that the former is more 'protected' from life because of its highly integrated nature.

Table 1

		Protestants	Catholics
Austria	(1852-59)	79.5	51.3
Prussia	(1849-55)	159.9	49.6
Prussia	(1869-72)	187.0	69.0
Prussia	(1890)	240.0	100.0
Baden	(1852-62)	139.0	117.0
Baden	(1870-74)	171.0	136.7
Baden	(1878-88)	242.0	170.0
Bavaria	(1840-56)	135.4	49.1
Bavaria	(1880-91)	224.0	94.0
Wuttemburg	(1846-60)	113.5	77.9
Wuttemburg	(1873-76)	190.0	120.0
Wuttemburg	(1881-90)	170.0	119

Suicides in Different Countries per Million Persons of Each Confession (Durkheim {1897} 1952:154)

Egoistic Suicide, Durkhéim considered, was largely an unavoidable off-shoot of the growth of moral individualism in modern society in which personal freedom and self-fulfilment are the primary values. So, if the Church wishes to re-form the social fabric of the nation it will need presumably to re-emphasise the value of strengthening social links whilst enabling the healthy development of personal identity.

Durkhéimian theories which remain at the level of group data can, in principle, predict the probability of suicide only in those social groups. They cannot say, for example, which particular individuals in any class, occupation or age group will be the ones to commit suicide, for that data on individuals are required.

So, Durkhéim's thesis concludes that suicide may be explained in terms of social causes that can manifest themselves as **collective** or **individual** forces. Also, that suicide varies then with the strength of the relational system in which the person is involved. Those deeply and intimately involved with others should be low suicide risks, and those isolated from meaningful relationships at higher risk.

(d) Social Factors

It is apparent that the incidence of suicide is influenced by factors external to the individual.   Figure 2 shows a marked decline during both world wars and a peak during the years of the depression in the early 1930's.   Interestingly, another low appeared in the 1970's, a time of greater affluence whereas there was a dramatic rise amongst men aged 25 to 54 years by 28% from 1,679 in 1981 to 2,143 in 1991, a period of high unemployment.

At the other end of the age scale 1995 saw 1014 people over the age of 64 take their lives, accounting for 17% of all suicide deaths.   The female suicide rate increases with age and the over 75's are particularly at risk and it is probable that bereavement, isolation, retirement and ill health are contributory factors.

Figure 2

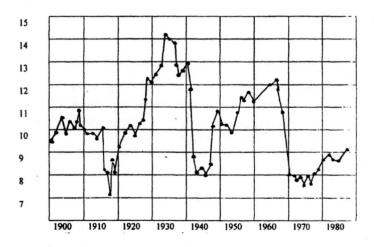

As we shall see, special factors like over-crowding and bullying in prisons (70 deaths in 1996) and the increasing problem of rural suicide (farmers are twice as likely to kill themselves as the rest of the population) point to the crippling despair and isolation that exists in these two widely differing environments. Accessibility of weapons in the last example and drugs (the medical profession have the highest occupation risk of suicide) point to a range of factors and practices that contribute to rises in suicide nationally.

But, of more pressing concern today is the question of employment as a possible factor. Attempts to detect a variation in SR across the range of employment status in the past have not been wholly convincing. Nevertheless, in 1997 it was found that 56% of young men and 40% of young women who attempted suicide had employment or study problems. (Samaritans, Exploring the Taboo 1997, see Table 2) The general impression gained from survivors was that long-term unemployment leads to illness often with psychiatric symptoms that might be associated with the suicidal.

Table 2
Problems reported at the time of attempt

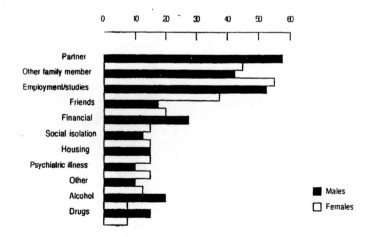

   Statistical examination can also tell us something about (i) the SR in
urban and rural populations and (ii) the methods used to commit suicide.
The most significant factors in the latter are those in determining the pain
involved and the availability of means. A look at the latest figures for 1996
(Table 3) show that for men, poisoning by exhaust gas and hanging are the
most common methods, probably because it is unlikely to fail and the means
are easy to provide.   The local profile reveals firearms and poisoning to be
equal in number to suicide by exhaust fumes, firearms would be found more
commonly in a rural area.

Table 3

Males

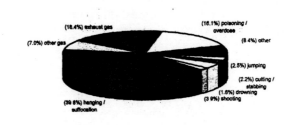

Females

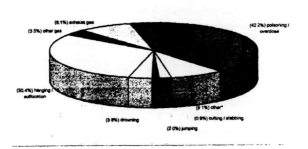

*includes shooting – 0.5%

9th April 1998   The Samaritans

(e) Summary

Durkhéim's influential work is important largely because it provides the first convincing examples of the methodical examination of statistical data as a means of exploring the social factors at play in human behaviour. I believe therefore, that a Christian response to suicide must take into account those elements of human living that can be said to be adversely affected by social conditions and change.

However, there is a danger of treating, simply, people's actions as rather complex forms of otherwise natural events. To constantly ascribe the existence of structural causes of suicide as the main factor in the confirmed growth of suicide nation-wide, is to neglect the individual characteristics of people.

Also, there is a limit to what general data can tell us about who may go on to commit the act. Unemployment is a good example. Though many are unemployed today it is difficult to draw a direct link between this condition and the actual numbers who commit suicide.

When we come to the discrepancy between the higher number of those who attempt suicide and the relatively small number who succeed, we may begin to realise that whilst undeniably there is sufficient data to argue that underlying social causes may contribute significantly to society-induced stress, there are also specific situational 'triggers' that need to be considered.

2. A Local Profile

It is very nearly a century since Durkhéim produced his influential study, and although there is continuing debate about his findings, it has nevertheless provided a backdrop of statistical research and methodology upon which more recent enquiry may be founded as well as contrasted.

What is important, however, regarding this investigation is that the human reality of suicide should also be explored within the context of local ministry so that considered Christian responses can take their departure from real life. It will be important also, to refer to official statistics (Government and Samaritan sources) as well as reflecting upon the latest National Health strategies that set challenging targets for the year 2000.

Finally, there may be useful contemporary research in our penal institutions that will offer further insight into the nature and plight of the vulnerable in society whilst helping to provide a variety of 'protecting agents' relevant to a Christian response.

In my local Deanery setting, where clergy and laity colleagues worked and worshipped, I felt it was crucial to gain some insight (reinforced with data where possible) into the extent and characteristic nature of suicide and self-harm that was currently presenting. Accordingly, I asked Chapter members to fill in a simple questionnaire, answers to which provided basic information based on the previous five years (see Appendix 1).

I focused on numbers, age and sex of victims and any salient features that may have contributed to their demise. My hope was that comparison of such data with the wider picture nationally might help identify underlying causes (some specific to a predominantly rural area) and any common 'triggers' that had precipitated these acts. Information such as this I conjectured, would be of great value at a later stage in the creation of a pastoral resource for clergy and laity and also in helping to provide a relatively simple model of local enquiry for those keen to minister in this field.

(a) Methodology

Pro-forma and individual profile forms were circulated to all clergy colleagues, requesting basic factual information on presenting suicides during a five year period. (see Appendix for specimen forms). To help the collation of observations, twenty areas of comment were indicated covering factors that are known from a wide body of research to be contributory. There was space for additional factors or features to be mentioned and respondents were instructed verbally to build up, where possible, a psychodynamic picture of the individual concerned. This information is tabulated on the following pages.

(b) Findings
(i) Age spread, sex and marital status

Nine areas reported one or more cases, a total of 22 cases (18 suicides and 4 attempted suicides), 11 were married, 9 were single, 1 widowed and 1 divorced. Ages ranged from 13 years to 78 years and consistent with national statistics there was a preponderance of males, 16 to 6 females (14 to 4 females completed suicides) a ratio of approximately 3:1. The average

age of this sample was 45 years for males (total for completed suicides) and 29 years for women (33 years for completed suicides).

Actual completed suicides showed 6 out of the 14 males were 22 years to 35 years and 8 out of 14 were 40 or older, whilst the 4 females were respectively 18, 30, 32 and 55 years of age. The 4 attempted suicides showed 2 females aged 14 and 25 years (wrist cutting) and 2 males aged 13 and 75 years (drugs). Figure 3 illustrates comparative death rates by age for England 1969-1991 shows female SR for the 15 to 24 years and 25-44 year groups have remained fairly static but the same groups for males have continued to rise alarmingly. In the Local Profile over half of male suicides (8 out of 14) were under 44 years, a figure which seems to mirror rises in these groups nationally.

Figure 1 shows suicide ebb and flow among both sexes between 1900 and 1991 in the United Kingdom. The female SR has fallen by 43% from 1981-1991 but in men it has continued to rise since the early 1970's (by 10% from 1981-1991). Normally, the largest number of male suicides occur in the 40-59 age group but the fastest growing SR of late has been in the under 25 age groups, suicide accounting for 20% of all deaths amongst young people (in the United Kingdom in 1995, 738 people aged between 15 and 24 took their lives), today is in the under 25 age groups (Samaritans, 1992).

Table 5 shows Suicide Trends for 1986 to 1996 though in fact in 1990 591 people under 25 killed themselves and in the last 10 years the SR has increased by 41% for the under 25's and by 74% for young men. Of the total young suicides, 80% are male and of young attempted suicides 80% are female. The recent find by the Samaritans (May 1992) that one in 100 girls aged 15 to 19 attempted suicide every year raises the very important issue of support and accurate data at secondary and tertiary levels of education (see Chapter 3) since 25% of those who call the Samaritans are under 25 years of age.

Figure 3

Suicide and Undetermined Deaths in the United Kingdom

	1988	1989	1990	1991	1992	1993	1994	1995	1996	1997	1998
Total	6872	6142	6468	6340	6398	6312	6129	6139	5881	5993	6182
#	12	11	11	11	11	11	10	10	10	10	10
+	15	13	14	14	14	13	13	13	12	13	13
MALE											
0-14	20	11	18	14	19	37	24	17	22	22	18
#	0	0	0	0	0	1	0	0	0	0	0
15-24	760	667	731	674	690	701	660	601	560	628	571
#	17	15	17	16	17	18	17	16	15	17	16
25-34	932	907	1031	1084	1061	1064	1189	1154	1153	1131	1316
#	22	21	23	24	23	23	25	24	24	24	28
35-44	949	841	931	997	972	915	899	956	852	880	971
#	24	21	24	25	25	23	23	24	21	21	23
45-54	663	644	723	770	776	769	732	725	740	777	772
#	21	20	22	23	23	22	20	20	20	20	20
55-64	624	549	530	478	519	510	465	463	422	435	477
#	22	19	19	17	18	18	16	16	15	15	17
65-74	482	398	430	343	393	374	342	336	342	292	302
#	22	18	19	15	17	16	14	14	15	13	13
75+	416	342	350	326	300	304	304	308	297	320	265
#	32	26	26	24	22	22	23	22	20	21	17
Male Total	4846	4359	4744	4686	4730	4674	4615	4560	4388	4485	4692
+	22	19	21	21	21	20	20	20	19	19	20
#	17	16	17	17	17	16	16	16	15	15	16
FEMALE											
0-14	5	12	4	9	10	13	15	15	9	13	7
#	0	0	0	0	0	0	0	0	0	0	0
15-24	182	164	142	160	151	142	117	139	149	138	159
#	4	4	3	4	4	4	3	4	4	4	5
25-34	244	261	263	247	284	274	269	242	269	274	255
#	6	6	6	6	6	6	6	5	6	6	6
35-44	313	249	273	251	248	262	252	294	262	293	271
#	8	6	7	6	6	7	6	7	7	7	6
45-54	312	291	275	274	284	267	239	269	272	276	250
#	10	9	8	8	8	7	7	7	7	7	6
55-64	310	287	251	242	242	204	210	192	170	183	177
#	10	10	8	8	8	7	7	7	6	6	6
65-74	341	245	268	233	231	218	183	197	170	175	186
#	12	9	10	8	8	8	6	7	6	6	7
75+	319	274	248	238	218	258	229	231	192	156	185
#	13	11	9	9	8	10	9	9	7	6	7
Female Total	2026	1783	1724	1654	1668	1638	1514	1579	1493	1508	1490
+	8	7	7	7	7	7	6	6	6	6	6
#	7	6	6	6	6	6	5	5	5	5	5

Figures in italics marked # indicate the rate per 100,000 population in the specific age group, figures
in italics, marked + indicate the rate per population over 14 years of age.

07/04/00   The Samaritans, 10 The Grove, Slough SL1 1QP
                                                                    www.samaritans.org

Table 4

(ii) Means Employed

Method	Males	Female	Total Number
Exhaust Fumes/Gas	4	-	4
Firearms	4	1 + 1 possibly murdered	6
Poison	4 (2 attempted)	2	6
Wrist Cutting	-	2 (both attempted)	2
Hanging	1	-	1
Drowning	1	-	1
Suffocation	1	-	1
Unclear	1	-	1
	16	6	22

In line with national statistics males predominantly chose suicides at later stages and were successful, mainly by exhaust fumes and poison, though an unusually high number chose firearms. Both female attempted suicides took recourse in wrist cutting, 2 completed suicides used drugs and one a firearm, considered a rare occurrence. The means of suicide is known to vary considerably between males and females: 34% of males poison themselves with exhaust fumes and a further 32% hanging. Among females self poisoning accounts for about 42% and in 30% cases hanging was the cause of death. (Table 3). The local profile shows a high number of males took drugs and used firearms whilst the figure for hanging was below average.

Significant Factors Represented

(i) Financial Difficulties

It is well documented that the suicide risk is greater where there are unhappy changes in financial circumstances. In this local survey three cases suffered intractable financial problems that were considered central to subsequent suicidal crises. Two males (1a) aged 51 years and (2b) aged 35 years owned businesses that had finally collapsed and in the first case bailiffs had visited the family home on the day of the suicide. Both men were secretive, the first a long standing church warden, failing to give away any sign of anxiety to his congregation.

The third case (5f) a female aged 32 years who died as a result of an insulin overdose attracted in addition a number of contributory factors: a difficult marriage settlement court case (the day preceding the act), one-parent responsibilities and the recent onset of diabetes. The accompanying financial morass, still being resolved today, was chronic and central to her demise. Financial difficulties were a significant factor in two other cases (6c) and (10a) and since it is not unusual for some victims to be particularly reticent about such problems, carers may need to raise such issues even at the risk of prying.

(ii) Marital Problems

Suicide risk is also greater where there is recent loss or break-up in a close relationship, especially marriage. Two cases, males aged 50 and 32 years (6c) and (3a) were experiencing marital problems. The first because of an imminent second divorce (see Chapter 3 illustration) the second because of the unwillingness of his wife to consider bearing children. In this survey a significant minority were suffering strained family relation-ships or a traumatic break-up preceding suicide. In this respect the fact that men reaching the age of 25 years are three times more likely to die by suicide if they are single, widowed or divorced, appears significant.

(iii) Unemployment

This survey identified 7 individuals who were unemployed and at risk because of business collapse, disablement and accommodation problems. The pernicious effects of unemployment, even for one year, are well researched: Platt, S. and Kreitman, N. 1984 (a) (b)., and Brit. Journal of Psychiatry, 1992: 750-756 discuss at length the link between suicide in young unemployed men and mental instability, especially those already under stress.   As early 1978 unemployment was seen as triggering psychological changes amongst jobless teenagers that could result in clinical depression, lethargy and insomnia, loss or gain of weight, suicidal thoughts, violent behaviour and greater dependence on alcohol or tobacco (Fagin 1978).

Four cases in this survey were men who had retired, the loss of a core activity that can put some at risk. Statistics are difficult to analyse precisely but research found that unemployed men were two to three times at greater risk of suicide than the average (Fox and Shawry, 1988) and one study found that they had an attempted suicide rate twelve to fifteen times higher than the employed, the rate being higher for those unemployed for longer than a year. (Hawton and Rose, 1986) See Figure 4.

Figure 4

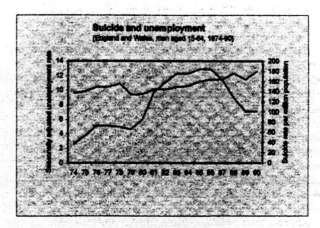

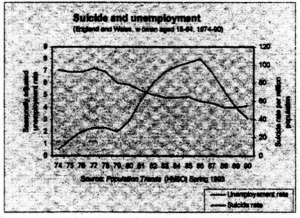

Table 5

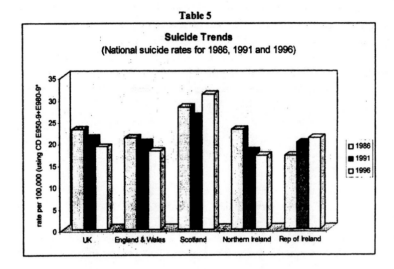

(iv) The Elderly

In July 1992 Virginia Bottomley, JP, MP, Secretary of State for Health, published a strategy for health in England entitled *The Health of the Nation* (HMSO, 1992: 118) In it we read of new targets for the reduction of suicide by the year 2000 (updated reduction 17% by 2010). In this connection mental illness is mentioned and it indicates that the prevalence of most types is just as high among the elderly as in the population as a whole.

However, depression, dementia and suicide are more common problems associated with bereavement and isolation as age increases. This fact has been known since the 1960's (Gibbs, J.P. and Martin, W.T., 1964, also Shulman, 1978:201) and earlier still Durkhéim ([1897] 1952:219) recognised that loss of material status influences highly, suicide among the elderly.

There were eight cases in this survey at age 50 or older (5d) suffering a long illness and (6a) recovering from the death of his wife with a diagnosis of terminal cancer to face. Among psychological effects, depression is thought to underlay two-thirds of elderly cases (Gurland et al, 1983: 55) exacerbated by negative evaluation of one's life in old age and lack of a supportive network.

Since there is likely to be a high risk of physical illness in the elderly it will always be important to combat this with regular medical examination and to lessen loneliness and isolation with its accompanying psychiatric symptoms. Easing of economic problems and retirement-related stress by social planning with more aggressive diagnosis and treatment of depression, will make for a more proactive style of prevention (Schneidman, 1985: 225) in which a parochial contribution may be significant.

(v) The Young

Though *The Health of the Nation* report (HMSO, 1992: 117) recognises there is

......increasing evidence that early effective intervention in childhood and adolescence can be important in preventing mental ill-health.

no official data exists to estimate the incidence of suicide or parasuicide (non-fatal acts of deliberate self-harm), in school situations. Whilst we may agree that the mental health of the young is important as many are vulnerable in addition to physical, intellectual, emotional, social or behavioural disorder *One Year On* (HMSO 1993:82) has yet to receive the results of a newly-commissioned national research review of mental health services for children and young people.

How this will utilise the natural education setting of the school in developing a critical philosophy of death and death risk for young adolescents has yet to be seen. Clearly, there is much to be learned, suicide is the third most common cause of death among young people and available estimates taken from the *Hospital In-patient Enquiry* up to 1985 report as many as 200,000 cases in a year.

Unlike suicide, which increases in incidence progressively with age, deliberate non-fatal self harm is most common among young adults. Here females out-number males by a ratio of 2:1 and among adolescents by a ratio of as many as 9:1. Nevertheless the rate of attempted suicide in young men has doubled in 10 years and making a suicide attempt increases a person's chances of eventually dying by 100 times. (Hawton, K. "Suicide and attempted suicide" in Handbook of Affective Disorders). Both females of the 4 parasuicides in this survey (2a) and (5g) cut their wrists and both were low in esteem with accompanying relationship problems. The 13 year old boy (6a) had been molested years earlier in a school situation and was struggling to share these confidences with his parents. (See Chapter 3 illustration).

(vi) Isolation

This local survey revealed that approximately half of cases and all of the 4 parasuicides showed degrees of isolation. Few adolescents escape the pain of loneliness and as an affective disorder it has been linked to a number of serious problems that include drug/alcohol abuse, delinquency, academic failure and suicide (Klerman, 1986:40; Pelan and Perlman, 1982)

Weiss (1973:35) has described a pattern of apathy, regret, helplessness and despair that can result from various forms of isolation:

Emotional Isolation - primarily the absence or loss of attachment figures at a time when adolescents are vulnerable.

Social Isolation - which stems from a lack of social integration with peer network or community.

Spiritual Loneliness - is a term used by a number of writers (Buhler, 1969: 167; Gaer, 1976) to describe the isolation that results from perceived deficits in the 'meaning' of a person's life.

Existential Loneliness - stems from an awareness of separateness, mortality and finiteness.

A number of researchers (May, 1953 and Yalon, 1980) describe adolescents who experience panic and despair as they struggle for autonomy and independence as a result of an absence of meaningful relationships. Guidance from mentors, teachers and clergy can be helpful in enabling the insecure adolescent to meet the challenge. Adolescents are vulnerable to situational changes that disrupt their relationships (divorce, break-up with friends, change of school) and they will typically adopt self-defeating interpretations of new experiences and become sensitive to criticism. Research shows that such loneliness is often at the centre of fractured strategies. (See Chapter 3 illustration).

(vii) Long-term Problems

This is an area where a Christian response can be particularly relevant in mobilising practical measures or long-term support. The 13 year old parasuicide (6a) had carried his secret for at least three years with carers suspecting but not able to identify the specific problem. Those that did know failed to inform parents and the adolescent took drugs out of desperation (this case Illustrated in Chapter 3). The 43 year old male suicide (8a) happened after 12 years of unresolved bereavement, those suffering long illnesses (5d) and the absence of a long-term relationship (8a) and (5g) are especially prone to suicide.

It is known that individuals often reveal suicidal feelings by talking about isolation, lack of hope and self-worth (Samaritans, 1992:8) and contrary to popular opinion those who talk about suicide will often go on to make an attempt. At least a quarter in this profile talked before their attempt and another quarter were intensely secretive about their intentions though signals were detectable to the vigilant observer. (Isolated life-style of (8a) and (6d); meticulous preparations of (5f); secretive about financial problems (1a) and (2b); case (5e) actually reading about 'life after death')

(viii) Accessibility of means and vulnerable occupations (Table 3)

The link between means and occupations is significant. The medical professions are twice as likely to kill themselves as the rest of the population. (Table 6 and 7) Farmers and their workers are next with suicide the second major cause of death for those under 45 years. The Samaritans (1992:6) have estimated that on average four farmers a week in England and Wales take their own lives and women married to farmers have a rate more than 20% above the average.

Both groups have been targeted by the Samaritans (Rural Outreach Programme launched Spring 1993). The latest data (Population Trends 1993, Table 7) considered that high stress, life and death decision-making, easy access to means and professional/social isolation is significant factors.

Table 6

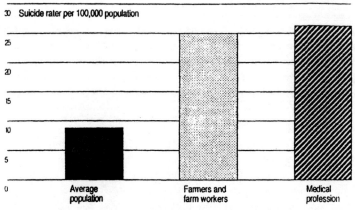

Source: OPCS Survey of Occupational Mortality, Great Britain 1979-80, 1982-83

Table 7

**Suicide by occupation:
the ten highest**

(England and Wales, male deaths
at ages 16-64. 1979-90

Occupation	PMR	No deaths
Vet	364	35
Pharmacist	217	51
Dental Pract'ner	204	39
Farmer	187	526
Medical Pract'ner	184	152
Therapist	181	10
Librarian	180	30
Typist, secretary	171	16
Social scientist	179	11
Chemist	169	70

Source: *Population trends* (HMSO)
Spring 1993

Possible Factors
High stress
Life and death decisions
Access to means
Isolation

PMR: proportional Mortality Ratio - the extent by which Suicide is more or less frequent compared to the population as a whole (100 = average)

Since this local profile is based on a predominantly rural environment it is important to take into account factors associated with its main occupation - agriculture. The uncertainty of change, an underlying cause in farming, triggers stress that can play havoc with mental and physical health, economic efficiency and most of all relationships. There are four factors however, which affect all farmers to some effect:

Economic Pressures - that affect not just the efficiency of the farm but those resources that enable a full and varied life.

Political Uncertainty - like medics, farmers are subject to decisions which may not be fully understood and they tend to be resistant to change.

Physical Isolation - over 14,000 workers left the agricultural industry in 1992 and with increased mechanisation a decrease in work force makes for fewer team-working activities.

Cultural Isolation - population turnover in rural areas has left the farmer relatively isolated. Squeezed between the hard realities of their existence and the demands of newcomers, who often convey a poor understanding and sensitivity to the rural life, isolation may be simply reinforced.

Following the disastrous BSE crisis in cattle 1997 The Rural Stress Information Network report that: farm incomes are down by up to 47%; proposed changes to the Common Agricultural Policy are causing undue tensions; farming enterprises generally are depressed and future uncertainties are exacerbated by the 'demonisation of farmers' by media and in the public eye.

(ix) Previous Health Problems

The local profile revealed that half of cases showed evidence of previous health problems including one case of schizophrenia, one of terminal cancer, five of depression some with psychiatric symptoms, one permanently disabled, one diabetic and one emphysema/asthma. There was also some evidence of drug or alcohol abuse in a quarter of cases and the relationship between this and suicide is strong. One study (Hawton et al, 1989) suggests that 15% of alcoholics may die by suicide and in addition during the last 25 years drug related deaths by suicide have increased sixfold for men aged 15 to 24 years and five-fold for men aged 25 to 44 (Population Trends, 1993).

The Health of the Nation white paper concerns itself with encouraging healthy life styles for those suffering mental illness, anxiety and depression, reducing the overall suicide rate by 15% and the suicide rate of the severely mentally ill by 33% (Figure 5). To achieve this all caring organizations must play their part in improving health, disseminating accurate information and working together in mutual alliances (Christian counselling organisations, house groups, and outreach initiatives).

Figure 5

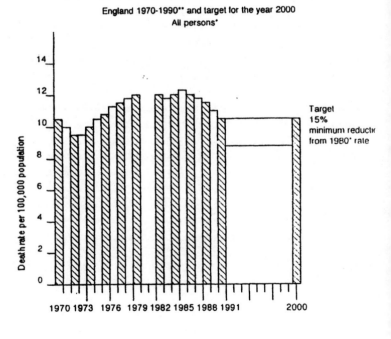

Death rates for Suicide and Undetermined Injury

England 1970-1990** and target for the year 2000
All persons*

The mental health charity MIND, which works for the right of people in mental distress to lead active and valued lives in the community, reports that every year six million cases of mental distress are diagnosed in England and Wales. Since 1946 there has been a 65% increase in first time referrals to psychiatric hospitals and with one person in four suffering from mental distress in their lifetime, everybody has a personal interest in making sure that support services are the best of their kind.

The Church is in a strong position in the community to help enhance these initiatives by development of its own network of concern and monitoring. It can do this by: **Self Help** - bringing people together to share the common problems of the sick by nurturing a greater awareness at all levels; **direct service provision** - counselling, visiting, befriending, helping the isolated; **community help** - clergy and laity playing their part as informed/concerned church agencies in liaison with G.P./Social Services panels and other voluntary organisations; finally **raising the issues** - by ensuring that health messages as conveyed via church media are accurate, constant and clear.

(d) Summary

Of course, to make real and co-ordinated progress in these four areas will require the lead and support of senior churchmen and women and provision of some Diocesan funding. The setting up of a human resource similar to that which exists here in the Oxford Diocese (SASH) can both serve and spearhead pastoral outreach encouraging a more effective parochial network of concern and support. SASH (Suicide and Self-harm, see Apprendix 4) exists to:

1. Support clergy and others who are pastorally involved in situations involving suicide self-harm.
2. Raise awareness of the problems of stress, depression and suicide so that the church is better informed.
3. Compile resources, especially liturgical, that will be of assistance to anyone involved in taking the funeral of a suicide victim.
4. Organise training for those interested in mental health issues. Today clergymen and women themselves require greater levels of support, especially in rural areas. Since there are now greater responsibilities than ever before for more churches, which

inevitably means significant increases in services, visiting, church council meetings and administration.

Our first priority is to raise the issue and make known the facts to all parishes, if possible with a Deanery breakdown of numbers presenting themselves to ministers over a period of time. Then the significance of ministry to the anxious, despairing and isolated needs to be highlighted as an important part of the pastoral commission of the whole Church.

Preaching and prayer/discussion groups might also include this issue as a regular topic for debate - i.e. the value of life/the waste of premature death; the sociological and psychological factors in spiritual health; what does the Bible tell us about life and death; the importance of these concepts for the young in Sunday schools and Confirmation preparation.

What would be needed at parish level would be a small pastoral group of individuals who themselves, by virtue of their own concerns and experiences and with the support of a Diocesan resource, could help offer insight, literature and basic knowledge on the hidden tragedy of suicide and depression.

Apart from the most common sociological factors associated with suicide, mental health has attracted immense problems of stigma and discrimination. The Church, as part of those caring services, can through its conveying of the Gospel message of healing acceptance, help a greater and more sensitive understanding.

Also, in a practical sense, they too can play their part in early detection of suicidal crises. A high number of these who go on to suicide have contacted a GP or health professional only weeks before. Time that might be employed in counselling is always at a premium in our medical services, therefore, the listening ministry as part of a parish resource may be more forthcoming.

Simon Armson, the editor of *The Samaritan News* (Spring 1993) writes in response to government recommendations that "the opportunity to form a partnership with health social care is a vital one." The Samaritans have existed for more than forty years (a total of 10,000,000 hours listening to the suicidal) offering complete and utter confidentiality with non-judgemental and non-directive support (the volume of calls has risen by 23% in the past decade, 22% of first time callers were under 25 and 8% over 60 – Listening Out Samaritan Paper 1994).

Nevertheless, of all the calls received in 1991, 42% were silent calls (33% in 1996) where no contact was established. There exists therefore, a tremendous need for others to listen also. Indeed, we may be in danger of being complacent in imagining that only the Samaritans can offer time to really listen to all the confusion, despair and emptiness of the suicidal.

In truth, what is needed is the emotional space, love and encouragement to enable the expression of such painful feelings. Also, it is important not to forget those who care for mentally sick people at home. To give them support, clergy and laity require informed education, insight and knowledge theologically of what their attitude might be to those driven to or contemplating suicide, it is the purpose of this Handbook to help meet this need.

3. Suicide in Prison - Lessons to be learned?

The role of the Chaplaincy in relation to prison suicide prevention tends to be restricted to ministering to the bereaved or visiting those who have made suicide attempts. But their potential significance is far greater than this. As listeners, they carry both a responsibility and a capacity to facilitate an environment in which listening and talking is possible.

(Liebling, A and Krarup, 1993: 144)

If there is something to be learned from recent experiences in prison, which saw major increases in suicide mainly amongst those on remand, it is the importance in our parochial ministry to "facilitate an environment in which listening and talking is possible." The absence of such interaction in our communities and congregations will surely negate the most powerful weapon in the Christian's armoury - the power to listen with congruence, empathy and unconditional positive regard to those who may be contemplating suicide. Such listening has been identified by both the Samaritans and prison authorities as the one most exciting development in the initiatives directed only recently towards the reduction of suicides in penal institutions.

The phenomenon of suicide in prison can provide important insight since 'poor copers' inside tend to consist of people who are also poor at coping in the community as well. For what results from a number of scientific researches is a clear picture of a type of prisoner, who is not dissimilar from the mainstream prison population, but who comes to prison with a history of general 'vulnerability' which is going to make his/her experience of custody not only difficult but a potential risk. (Liebling, A. and Krarup, 1993:70).

It is from a deeper understanding of this vulnerable group that a Christian response can learn, in part, to build up knowledge so as to better develop strategies through a ministry of 'active listening'. Because prison officers and chaplains have daily contact with 'poor copers' their observations and knowledge of behaviour are extremely valuable to us as we attempt an informed response to suicide in the community.

First, it is necessary to address the fact that incidents of self-injury have increased over the past ten years. According to the Home Office there were 2,963 recorded incidents in 1991 and almost half (1,208) were committed by prisoners under or aged 21 years. (Howard League, 1993: 28-30). Like the population outside, the largest proportions were to be found in the 21-25 years and 26-30 years age groups, arguably the most 'prison prone' age group. (See figure 6). Already by 1969 suicide rates in prison exceeded those in the general population by about 4:1 and by 1979 this had risen to 6:1 (Topp D. 1979; Home Office, 1984)   Total deaths for 1997 was 70 (Suicide Awareness Support Group, Samaritans)   (See Table 8).

Table 8

In 1997 there were 70 self-inflicted deaths in prisons in England and Wales, 67 men and 3 women. This figure is a 9% increase on the previous year, a 40% increase since 1990 and a 159% increase since 1983. However, the *rate* of self-inflicted deaths in prisons in England and Wales is currently 115 per 100,000 population, a slight decrease from 116 per 100,000 in 1996. Nonetheless, the rate of suicide in prisons in England and Wales is currently over six times the total male suicide rate and nearly ten times the rate for both sexes for this region. 39% of those who took their own lives in prison were on remand.

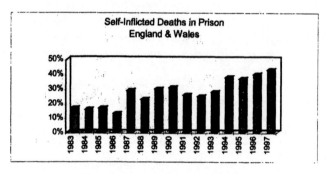

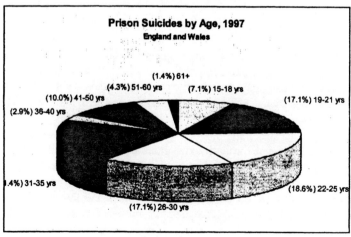

The thrust of much of the existing research has been to identify characteristics or factors associated with suicidal prisoners in order to predict who might be at risk. This approach suffers from a number of limitations: the risk factors tend to be shared by large numbers of prisoners, resulting in a large number of false positives (inmates considered at risk who do not subsequently kill themselves), Also, there were difficulties inherent in the risk identification process, for example Dooley (1990:40) found that only 16% of those who committed suicide between 1972 and 1987 had been identified as at risk by staff.

These limitations led to greater emphasis being given to the possible situational and motivational components of self-injury. It was felt that such an approach would be more likely to yield information to use in planning intervention strategies than the traditional prediction approach. Liebling and Krarup (1993) see a distinct community dimension to the prison suicide problem, it seems to be increasing in a context of significantly increased levels of suicide in particular 'prison prone' groups in the community itself, especially the 'poor copers'.

Many of the factors associated with prison suicides appear to have their original source in the community: social and economic disadvantage, a general and increased sense of vulnerability and isolation amongst the young in modern society, loss of ties, alcohol/drug abuse and lack of a realistic future. In addition, there exists publicly a good deal of denial where, although suicide rates are seen as a problem in the young and the old (Dickstra, 1996) there is little reported in the popular press and little being done in terms of allocating budget resources for prevention.

In other words the prison data mirrors to some extent the community situation, underlying causes remaining significant in both though triggers are clearly more precipitive in penal institutions. Prison medical officers now consult risk indicators, which include drug/alcohol abuse, history of psychiatric problems, non-contact with family and symptoms of anxiety to help in their assessments (Guidelines C.I. /1989)

Perhaps the most important finding is that suicides in prison, like those on the outside, are not primarily a psychiatric problem but more a problem of coping. In Chapter 3, I shall be discussing the significant need for 'sustaining external resources' (Maltsberger, 1986: 17-29) that aid 'poor copers' in the wider community. In prison they fall into the following categories, though they are paralleled to some extent in the community.

- domestic (isolation, relationships)
- situational (victimisation, regime frustration)

- strategic (practical needs, accommodation)
- emotional (depression, fear guilt)
- medical (psychiatric/physical condition, alcohol and drugs)
- other reasons (low esteem, worthlessness)

'Protecting agents' which have helped mitigate against suicidal feelings in prison may also be applicable to the community.

- visits/contact with family
- constructive occupation of time
- improved accommodation
- support from meaningful others, chaplain, prison visitors, clergy, neighbours, etc.
- closer monitoring of health needs
- opportunities to talk in a friendly, supportive environment.

But by far the most influential development on all fronts has been the development of a pioneering 'prison branch' of the Samaritans that followed the tragic death of 15 year old Philip Knight in 1991. There are now a number of Samaritan trained prisoners who will share a cell with anyone suffering a suicide crisis until it subsides and they are always on hand to listen in confidence and privacy. (Swansea Prison)

Since 1991 the numbers of self injuries in this prison has halved and there have been no deaths. The listener scheme thrives as a direct result of the partnership of effort between staff, prisoners and Samaritans and indeed it may provide part of the answer in a Christian response to suicide in the community.   Today there are Samaritan supported listener schemes in 98 prisons of every category and they form a significant part of Prison Service Strategy.

Clearly, listening to others as human souls, i.e. as people "as God might see them" (Liebling, 1993:80) encouraging others to "sit where they sit" is crucial. Such work, however, cannot be undertaken without real 'knowledge' and experience (which is where prisoners who have been victims themselves are so effective).

The process that has emerged being to look something like this:

Support means Time, Trust and Understanding
|
Through active listening and befriending with others to help
|
Widening perspective with 'support groups'
|
Attention to health, accommodation, future direction

I believe reassurance about God's ultimate love to all souls is vitally important but conveyed by action as well as in words, the aim being to encourage the individual to realise that they are not alone.   So far as young suicide attempters are concerned, relationships with partners or family are most often mentioned as problems and there is research to indicate that adolescent attempters report less perceived support and understanding from their parents than adolescents who are depressed (Keinhorst et al. (a) 1995).

Clearly, parental relationships are a very important factor and a majority of adolescent suicide attempters grow up in families with much turmoil (often broken by death or divorce) made worse by unemployment, illness or addiction.   In Chapter 3, I wish to examine to what extent early psychodynamic development within the family has played a part in rendering some individuals to overwhelming stress and anxiety. For if this is the case, then an understanding of the processes involved may aid the development of any therapeutic relationship between carer and victim.

CHAPTER THREE

SUICIDE - A QUESTION OF PSYCHODYNAMIC DEVELOPMENT

1. Vulnerability to Suicide and a Pastoral Response

In Chapter Two we have concerned ourselves with influences on perceived suicide rates by underlying social causes, structural defects that contribute to a stressed society. In Chapter Three, I propose to examine other factors of a psycho-dynamic nature that from an early age may have contributed to the vulnerability of individuals. It is my belief that various psychological 'triggers', sometimes the direct result of poor parenting and much of it located in the social systemic context of the family and other wider relationship networks, may well contribute to subsequent suicidal crises. From the local profile, I will present two case illustrations, with which I am familiar, to highlight the variety and nature of such problems.

In addition it will be important to draw a distinction between suicide and non-fatal, but deliberate, self-harm when looking at the formulation of suicide risk and therefore I shall examine, briefly, framework for a school-based initiative to combat the numerous parasuicides common amongst the young.

But first, what of the pastoral response? Even though I had, as a pastor and before, known a number of people who subsequently committed suicide, I realised soon after that I was unprepared for the challenge of Renton's case, to whom this enquiry is dedicated. The nigh insuperable problem was that he was my brother and therefore it was difficult to maintain an objective, caring and balanced approach to his tragic circumstances. Knowing his manner of responding to people, his desire on the one hand to be accepted as worthy, competent and appreciated and on the other his intense anxiety and lack of self-esteem, created an impossible dilemma for one so close.

However, since he had few friends it was important not to turn him away, though I could not erase past images of him as a selfish, self-centred person significantly lacking in control, yet sickeningly dependent upon his mother. Though I felt compassion for him, nevertheless I was at heart, critical and sometimes unsympathetic, resorting to 'pep talks' and gratuitous advice rather than listening attentively in a non-directive way.

Pastoral care, as I understand it, is about a relationship with another and for it to be truly loving and caring it requires not only honesty but also integrity because so often those who seek help at distressing points in their lives are hoping that **our** faith will somehow help them and restore hope. Certainly I offered understanding and help, but I needed to offer more, a real identity with his desolation, vulnerability and despair.

Our integrity requires an essential empathy and to do this we need to act from our 'wholeness' as human beings, i.e. from our inner selves. This I suspect was not so in my case, it was less painful to take refuge in practical advice and even criticism rather than to recognise that his life was disintegrating because of his intrinsic vulnerability.

Also, pastoral care is grounded not so much in expertise but in mutuality and this can be uncomfortable for the minister, who may be tempted to direct so as to 'control' developing situations, sometimes as a means of protection. What is needed, is to share our common humanity, our sense of meaning rooted in out belief in transcended humankind through the resurrection of Christ so that others who have lost our sense of wholeness may derive courage and hope.

In retrospect, I realise I was no better than Renton, I too had suffered similarly the ravages of our upbringing together and I was no wiser or more deserving. I was merely more sustained with a life of meaning that derived from a real sense of grace through a Saviour who had suffered to the end ('My God, my God, why hast thou forsaken me? (Mk.15:34)

I believe, not with guilt but with regret, that my concern was principally one of competence to deal with Renton rather than any genuineness of response. Clearly, even in the light of recent research on contributory factors, offering advice however practical will not of itself encourage hope. Rather, listening and absorbing the words of another with complete acceptance has to be the psychodynamic environment in which God's love can reach the other. Preoccupation with the outcome (unless dangerously imminent) ought not to be our chief concern, ours is to be a channel for the Holy Spirit.

The primary pastoral image for me has always been, quite naturally, that of the Shepherd, one who actively looks for those that are lost (Ez.24) and shows concern for those who have strayed. (Matt.18:12-14) In a suicidal crisis, however temporary, the victim can be said also to have lost their way, their life losing its meaning or direction. So the pastoral care of the Good Samaritan (Luke 10:30-37) and the ability to lead by example (1Peter,5:2) which we see in the model of Christ the Good Shepherd (John10:1-18) seems particularly appropriate.

Such Shepherding, to use an educational maxim, is fundamentally 'leading from the known to the unknown', from pain and anguish to light and meaning. Leadership such as this requires to be expressed with great sensitivity drawing on not only our experience but that of others, however painful the exploration. Later, I shall be arguing that where there is little direct knowledge, then training and information must be provided for those who may be called upon to minister in such a situation.

There is another image, however, that is equally relevant to cases such as Renton's: the image of the 'wounded healer'. (Wright, 1982). Ministering to those who are driven to contemplating self-destruction will naturally provide a desire to retreat in the fact of such an abrogation of life. Yet, we are wounded too. Though we desire to bring healing, we also bear the scars of living. So it is that Christ provides the definitive model of utter vulnerability and weakness in the human frame of Jesus. Here can be seen the power of God at work.

This model, I now realise, was beyond my conception in 1992. The notion that as we have a share in Christ's many sufferings so also through Christ we can share in God's help (2Cor.1:5f), has only now become a convincing testimony. Wounds, sometimes long-standing, are an important way into the helping of another, but first, they need to have been uncovered and dealt with in ourselves.

Once we have been enabled to come to terms with our own sufferings and needs, then we can be of real service to others, for such experience can be transformed by Christianity into qualities that can help us minister. In Gethsemane (Matt.26:38) Jesus asks his disciples to keep watch over him as he faces the horror of his fate, similarly we too may need to 'keep watch' over those crushed by the sickness of spirit called despair.

The 'wounded healer' gains not only strength but the appropriate response to others by acknowledging weakness and hurt. Having entered the depths of our own experience of loss and pain and having found hope, we can truly empathise with the other. Pastoral care, I believe, does not remove pain, as if the shepherd has found the stray now making it secure, but it can transform crippling anxiety and fear, absorbing anger and rage. It is transformed both by **acceptance** and then by being **shared.**

We now know that most people who are suicidal are not so much psychiatrically ill but despairing, so they are able to register the love and concern of another where it is authentic, though it may mean not only staying close but also enabling the other to reject and let go of us.

In Renton's case, I believe this indeed is what happened. Though sincerely meant, my pastoral care was supportive and even practical, but it lacked knowledge and experience and it was not sufficiently rooted in my own understanding of pain. The case illustration that follows is an attempt to paint, as objectively as possible, the circumstances that led to Renton's demise, together with appropriate analysis based on recent theories of psychodynamic development. This knowledge has not only informed understanding of my own inadequacies but widened my own perspectives, hence its inclusion here as a resource for those who seek to minister to the suicidal.

Case Illustration - Renton (6c)

Renton, elder son of two with a younger sister, was a 'war baby', his parents having married whilst both were serving in the army. He was born out of wedlock and his father was divorced, theirs was a most unhappy marriage. For the first six years Renton was brought up by a variety of 'aunties' within his father's family, his mother servicing several family homes in exchange for board and lodgings.

From the beginning he was not wanted and his birth was not planned. The relationship between his parents was strained providing very little cohesive support. Though he appeared to be the 'centre of attraction' the attention seemed superficial and lacked continuity. Older members of the family consider that he sustained considerable emotional injury during these formative years, consequently he was not enabled to deal adequately at a later stage with the anxiety of separation with all the emotional dangers of aloneness.

In 1947 mother and child returned to the North of England, father having left home, but after some financial difficulties he returned and a further boy and girl were born. For the next twenty years the family stayed together but always with physical violence between parents and Renton as an over-demanding older son.

Curiously, in spite of a notable absence of demonstrative affection between Renton and his mother, he clung to her even when she also threatened to leave the family 'for good'. She insisted however that his father should take his responsibilities and remain. He had been a good soldier, but in civilian life he was a steel worker, an illiterate, inward-looking and moody individual who took to smoking and drinking as his recreational activities.

Father and son hardly ever spoke to one another and Renton, highly susceptible to criticism, remained deeply influenced by his unpredictable mother. Renton remained very insecure, fearing the threatened loss of his mother. Though he did fairly well at school, eventually reading Theology at university, the decision was heavily influenced by his mother's ambition for him to be accepted by the Church.

As a youth he was fiercely aggressive, highly self-centred and inevitably wounded by any reproach from teachers or authority figures. He would fly into uncontrollable rages if he could not have his own way or if he was thwarted. He blamed his parents constantly for anything that went wrong in his life and he too, could be very violent. He was known to keep a sheath knife and, sometimes in tears, he would threaten to use it on himself.

His mother was constantly demanding the highest standards of achievement, appearing to live her life through the successes of her eldest son. He, seemingly could not escape her clutches though he did make the effort to go away to study, but the university he chose was rather too close. Theirs was a strange, symbiotic relationship. Renton lived with his mother most of this period, though it was an unsettled time of rages and tears. He found it difficult to mix with others, he was deeply unhappy and lonely, lacking self-worth and prone to anxiety about the least little problem,

It was surprising therefore, that in 1963 he joined the army (probably an idea derived from his parent's experience) rising quite quickly to the rank of Captain in the Education Corps. Somehow the structured, organised life in the armed services helped provide stability and much needed self-esteem. Nevertheless, five years later he resigned in considerable debt (he could not resist possessions of all descriptions from cars to expensive model aeroplanes) returning to a teaching post where he met his wife to be (a German national).

Marriage quickly followed, she was organised, hard-working and strong, and in a sense, resembled his mother. She found him charming though emotionally naive, sexually inexperienced and unable to relax or show his feelings. He remained fiercely loyal to his mother though admitting her neurotic tendencies. He was persuaded not to invite his father to the wedding.

A house was purchased that he characteristically attempted to make a 'perfect home' and he complained of being misunderstood and undervalued as a teacher. He impulsively rejoined the army and was posted to Germany, two children were born in quick succession during which time he became gradually more unstable and disturbed taking to drink and drugs.

He continued to be wearing to others, selfish with money, always having to be good at everything - skiing, singing, physical pursuits, etc.

Soon the marriage began to flounder, he became increasingly possessive of his wife and jealous of his very talented children. So after an acrimonious row with his Commanding Officer, who he said did not value him, they returned to England, Renton to a Deputy Headship in an ancient grammar school. He once again took refuge in a house cluttered with possessions remaining stable, so long as the school and its staff were overt in recognising his abilities. Privately, he was becoming violent and frustrated sexually. A final move to another senior teaching post, complete with 'dream house' triggered extensive anxiety and depression. On one notable occasion he went into the garden and burnt some treasured possessions, a spontaneous gesture of pain and loss of self.

He became very ill with extensive psychiatric symptoms and eventually his wife divorced him 'for the safety of the children', He entered a period of extraordinary self-delusions and intractable panic (following the stock market collapse of 1987 he had lost collateral and this preyed on his mind). He finally lost his job after he was accused of molesting a female pupil on a school holiday and he was 'retired on grounds of ill-health', his life in ruins.

Over the past few years we had spoken at length about suicide for he was uncertain about his desire to continue living. On the one hand he wanted to change but on the other his need for attention and love from others (there were few friends left) demanded that he direct his rage at all those who he considered had 'ruined his life'. After two attempts on his life he finally succeeded in 1992.

The letters he left (he was a prolific letter writer) express anguish, blame and revenge on those who had not remained loyal. He felt dishonoured, ill and ashamed but also incredibly angry. He seemed unable to pin point when everything had begun to go wrong, memory of his youth was vague, as he said, he had always felt 'doomed'.

He told me a few days before of what his intentions were, and I spoke to him of a fresh start and of hope, but he clearly did not have the resources within himself to cope with such chronic problems of self-hate, anxiety and overwhelming stress. I assured him that I would not be judgmental and we agreed that a God of love is a God who will always be close wherever there is human pain and anguish. Christianity teaches that Jesus understood the loneliness of those who felt God-forsaken and I assured Renton that this was my belief also. Now, I look back and I see, that at a critical time in Renton's development he was forsaken by the most important building block of all - human love.

To understand the vulnerability to suicide is to understand the psychology of despair   (Maltsberger, 1986:1)

Indeed there is a wide body of opinion to suggest that persons who suffer emotional injuries in childhood may later prove vulnerable to despair, especially in two areas of early development, namely mastery of anxiety and the regulation and maintenance of self-esteem. For the expression of despair has two distinct parts (i) a state of great emotional pain, so intolerable and unrelenting that it appears not to be endurable, and (ii) a growing certainty that life cannot go on. Such a state is distinguished by three basic conditions: aloneness, self contempt and murderous rage. I shall be referring to Renton's case as we explore these more fully.

(a) Aloneness

As a child matures towards adulthood a series of danger situations must be successfully mastered. At first the small infant grows alarmed if it senses that it is in physical danger, associating relief with the helping responses of mother. Very soon she is recognised as a separate person and the child begins to experience separation anxiety - vulnerability.

Freud ([1926] 1957:77-178) recognised that if the child is unrelieved or abandoned by its mother before it has the capacity to soothe its own distress when left alone, then it will become vulnerable to emotional disaster. Soothed, over time and in a consistent way, the child will build up its hope-giving experience, become tolerant of separation and can then cope with its own self. A child subject to many occasions of emotional danger (separation, violence, disturbance, lack of real identification with mother or father) will not develop an adequate capacity to respond to later distressing circumstances.

Renton's early development was similarly impaired. An insecure home-life, complete with the absence of one or other parent, lack of affection and continual strained relations, may have contributed significantly to his intense anxiety and poor self-image.

A number of researches (Mahlen, 1975: Bibring; 1953:13-48) recognise depression as symptomatic of such an ego state. Distinguished by a decrease of self-esteem and helplessness such inhibited functions arise especially when the ego is unable to achieve some aspiration, commonly a demand to be worthy, loved, competent and appreciated.

In Renton's case much of his anxiety seemed to be channelled into anger and wild tantrums and he seemed not to have adequately experienced a state of competence, peace and love in early life. He continued throughout his life to be unable to move away from his mother, toward whom much of his anger was directed.

If the individual cannot internalise these regulatory functions then he may need to seek regulation from some other potential external sustaining source such as a person, a pursuit or a way of life. In Renton's case this may have been his wife, his hobbies and his roles as soldier and teacher. Today, such emotional deprivation is thought to emanate directly from an 'impaired separating out of mother and child' in those early years. (Dockar-Drysdale, 1990)

(b) Self Contempt

To experience this sense of aloneness for a substantial period of time is to enter an empty, unreal world where one feels completely abandoned and worthless. Renton constantly reported feeling beyond love, he clung to his wife as he had to his mother taking comfort in the accumulation of possessions. But, to be so hopelessly alone also generates feelings of self contempt and discussion of this requires a little exploration of the super-ego and its work in the regulation of self-respect.

When an adult calms himself in the face of anxiety, he draws on his own mental resources previously learned from his mother, a well-established and internalised sense (super-ego). In the regulation of self-esteem the individual chastises himself from within the confines of his own mind, the super-ego formed from a mental representation of his mother.

It is noteworthy that the super-ego in suicidal individuals appears to be sometimes severely aggressive and perhaps many of them were neglected and deprived of consistent empathic contact as children (Firestone, 1997 a.b. 1998). Repeated frustration of emotional needs, as we see with Renton, can arouse great hostility which the suffering individual may have projected onto a parent, particularly if they are unusually critical or demanding (similarly with any other authority figure).

The super-egos of those with suicidal tendencies are often implacably critical and they are quick to self contempt, their consciences being extremely severe. So much so, that if the individual feels the impulse to hit out at a parent or authority figure, the conscience directs the hurt to itself as well.   At the end, Renton expresses blame as well as shame, revenge and dishonour.

(c) Rage

It is in this connection that the affect state of murderous rage may be significant. States of profound helplessness evoke primitive fight and flight reactions. The person who experiences aloneness or self contempt cannot, however, take flight and instead feels trapped and vulnerable to an intensely critical super-ego.

In children, separation panic can often be observed as fury when parents threaten to go away as Renton's parents did. Suicidally vulnerable adults, who have not mastered the developmental task of separation, can also experience attacks of murderous hostility when losses are threatened. Both Renton's wife and children had been threatened by him. Intense guilt may also supervene, the severity of the person's conscience demanding suicide as punishment.

Another function of the super-ego is that of caring and protecting the self (Freud, [1926]1957:141-207) suicidal people can be quite indifferent to their own welfare, seemingly having little capacity to award themselves love (Renton drank and took drugs). In so doing, the super-ego fails to invest the self with pride or satisfaction even when the individual attains something like the super-ego's expectations (graphically seen in Renton's 'perfectionism'). This may suggest that parent representations interjected in super-ego formation were ungenerous or unloving, or as in Renton's case, always demanding more and not rewarding. He was therefore, unable to develop a super-ego scheme which included representations of parents who loved, noticed and admired him.

When these experiences of aloneness, self-contempt and murderous hate are further exacerbated by the normal vicissitudes of life, pessimism and anxiety may give way to depression and despair, a vicious circle. Not unnaturally, such individuals are not only cruel to themselves but so often to those who become emotionally involved.

(d) Sustaining resources

In order to minimise distress the individual must rely on outside resources, however, the individual may become totally dependent on their continued support to sustain self-regard. Frequently, such persons want an exclusive relationship with their supporting other, and are quite unable to share (even with children) seeing it as near abandonment. We see this in Renton's case, where he became pathologically jealous of his children and aggressively dependent on his wife. Such demanding behaviour made him difficult to live with and his violence almost seemed to provoke the loss he most feared (like his mother's threats when he was a child). It is well documented that even so, many individuals can somehow manage, until there are other losses such as job, prestige, money or self-regard.

Suicides as a result of loss are very common, likely to take place in the context of divorce especially where there is alcohol or drugs involved. It is not so much the quality of the other but what they provide in the way of stability that is crucial. Renton also had very few close friends seeming to require no more than minor social contacts - what psychologists describe as 'part objects' which provide just sufficient support without requiring reciprocation.

Some individuals also depend on a cause or a group. In Renton's case, so long as the Commanding Officer or Headmaster's valuation could be maintained in some idealised form, then all was well. It only needed perceived repudiation from them for his vulnerability to be triggered. Work can provide a sustaining resource and Renton was very dependent upon this, its loss, however, with the attendant shame of a possible police case, helped to provoke a crisis.

The so-called 'cry for help' is often a bid to obtain a substitute resource in the face of loss. Renton made two attempts on his life and though relationships were offered he rejected them preferring only his wife, hence management of the crisis was especially difficult.

(e) The Suicide Crisis

As we have seen, vulnerability to suicide can arise from failure to develop satisfactory self-regulatory structures in early psychodynamic development. The individual is not psychiatrically ill but is vulnerable to the affects of anxiety and stress. Hence, where recourse has been made to external structures of self-regulation, then the individual may be overwhelmed by their loss, feeling worthless, alone and angry.

Clergy and laity who are befriending the suicidally vulnerable will need to be aware of these processes, not only gently uncovering them, but through counselling, enabling the individual to understand their own responses to perceived abandonment. Feelings of hostility, fury and anger need to be accepted and safely expressed, if not, suicide may well provide the channel instead.   Indeed, Freud (1957) describes suicide as the equivalent of killing someone else.

2. Non-Fatal Deliberate Self-Harm

All too often, attempted suicide is seen as failed suicide. However, annually 200,000 people (Samaritans, 1993) are estimated to make a 'deliberate non-fatal attempt on their lives, done in the knowledge that it was potentially harmful' (Morgan, 1979) Commonly this behaviour is used as an attempt at manipulation or to gain temporary relief from social problems. Typically an overdose or wrist cutting is used, the act being more impulsive than pre-planned.

It is clear that a previous suicide attempt is now considered to be a 'major predictive factor' in a completed suicide (Aldridge, 1998) along with social class, unemployment, previous psychological treatment, substance abuse and personality disorder (Hawton, Fagg and Hawkins 1993; Suominen et al. 1996).

Suicide attempts are higher among women than men with the highest rate among the young. More than 50% make more than one attempt (Aldridge, 1992; Stenager and Jenson, 1994; Wells, 1991) and of special concern, up to two-thirds consult a health and social welfare professional prior to making their attempt (Stenager and Jenson, 1994)

(a) Extent and Nature of the Problem

In truth, the current epidemic of self poisoning and injury presents a formidable challenge to society. Wexler et al (1978:1805) writes 'this phenomenon appears to be prevalent throughout the western world', the crises that lead to D.S.H. covering a wide range of life's problems, and often in people who have been made vulnerable by personal/social difficulties (though only a small minority of people can be said to be psychiatrically ill).

In fact, D.S.H. has become the most common reason for women admitted as emergencies in General Hospitals and the second most common reason for men after heart disease (ratio of 2:1 females to males and amongst adolescents 9:1, Samaritans 1993). There have been massive increases in England and Wales (Alderson, 1974:1050) and in the West (Weissman 1974:737). In Oxford, for example, there was a four-fold increase during the ten years to 1973 (Evans,1967; Bancroft, 1979) subsequently reaching a peak in the 1980's.   There exists also a clear correlation between medicinal poisoning and the prescribing of psychotropic drugs during those years (Forster, 1985:657-74).

It is clear that it is the young who are most at risk, particularly females between the ages of 15 and 19 years. Therefore, all those who are to care for the young need to have an understanding of the circumstances in which attempts occur. Most instances are preceded by stressful events which involve a key person, commonly a quarrel with a partner or a boy/girlfriend problem (adults who abuse or reject children have high rates of D.S.H. also, Roberts, J. and Hawton, 1980).

The most common problem identified among a series of 50 adolescents (of whom 45 were girls) aged 13 to 18 years who had taken overdoses was their relationship with parents, complaining particularly about their inability to discuss problems (See Case Illustration - Michael)   Hawton et. al., in their 1982 study found that 36% were living with one parent, 12% with neither parent and 12% had been in long term care with the social services. More than half had problems at school and half with personal relationships. There is commonly evidence of ill health, although actual psychiatric disorders are rare. (See Table 9 and Barraclough et. al., 1974:355-73)

Table 9
Current Problems Identified for 50 Adolescent Self-Poisoners

Problem Area	Percentage of Subjects for whom each problem was applicable %
Parents	76
School/work	58
Boy/girlfriend	52
Social Isolation	28
Sibling(s)	22
Physical Health	22
Psychiatric Symptoms	20
Sexual	16
Relationship with peers	14
Alcohol	14
Physical illness of family	14

It is not easy to establish why there is a preponderance of females among adolescent self-poisoners but research points to three areas (Hawton, 1986:253), (i) girls may mature and face problems of adulthood earlier than boys (ii) self-poisoning itself may be a more acceptable coping strategy for girls than boys and (iii) boys may have better outlets for dealing with distress, such as over-aggressive behaviour and alcohol abuse.

Statistics show a low incidence of suicide under the age of 14 years and this may be due to the fact that the concept of death develops later in childhood with full awareness of the implications not being gained until early adolescence. From an educational viewpoint, it is likely that little exploration of such a concept takes place in secondary education or in church circles. Such work could be undertaken by clergy and teachers in anticipation of relevant questioning by adolescents (Kocher, 1974:404-11). Another factor is the relative rarity of depression in young children, since there needs to be a marked degree of cognitive maturation before a child feels and understands the concepts of despair and helplessness.

An alarming fact is that, of those who commit D.S.H., about 15-25% are re-admitted to hospitals within twelve months and this may be due initially to poor follow-up counselling, but also, because of the presence of long-lasting social and personal problems (Morgan et. al. 1975:361). This is seen as a serious defect in care since there exists an increasing risk of dying with repetition of the act. Eventually, individuals can become chronic repeaters with a lifestyle which is disorganised, often seeking attention or temporary relief through drugs or alcohol. A typical circle of hopelessness can ensue (see below) (Vaughan 1985)

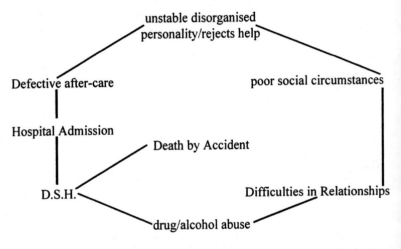

Carers can help at all points: hospital admissions noted and taken seriously; providing after-care as a team including counselling and pastoral support; befriending and actively working to improve social conditions; warning against dangers of drugs/alcohol.

In addition, it is important to remember that many people who poison/injure themselves have been in contact with potential helping agencies shortly before they carried out their acts.   Bancroft et. al. (1977:289-303) researched 141 such people to establish time of last contact (Table 10). Results given in percentages.

Table 10

Helping Agency	Contact made within 1 week	Contact made within 1 month
	%	%
GP	36	63
Psychiatrist	15	22
Social Worker	10	22
Clergy/Voluntary agency	13	23
Samaritans	4	6
Any Agency	54	82

Most common was the GP since many of the sample were suffering from anxiety/ depression associated with social/inter-personal difficulties. Sadly, psychotropic drugs were often prescribed, many of which may be used in subsequent attempts. Psychiatrists had seen marginally more than clergy/voluntary agencies, but the Samaritans had seen only a small percentage (Kreitman, N. and Cowdry, 1973:1-8). Hawton K. and Bladstock (1976:571) found similar data but noted that the younger age group consulted the GP less often than might have been expected tending to perceive him 'as being disapproving, unsympathetic or too busy.'

In her book, The Long Sleep – Young People and Suicide (1995) Kate Hill writes that the GP's skill in 'recognising and responding to depression and suicide risk is vital to suicide prevention, since it is usually GP's who treat mental health problems, including 95% of reported depression. Yet experience in mental care (or psychiatry) is not, at present, a compulsory part of the GP's training. (Hawton, 1994)

It seems clear that most individuals at risk do communicate their intentions beforehand and often to several people. From a Christian view point therefore, we must ask ourselves whether we are listening at every level, raising the issue sufficiently in Church Publications, Church Councils and emphasising that where there is depression, anxiety, major change and relationship problems, there will always be the very real risk of D.S.H. Above all, pessimism about the future itself, should be recognised as a major cause for it has been suggested that hopelessness as a symptom rather than depression is the more significant factor (Beck et.al., 1975:285).

Once again, like suicide, D.S.H. has a close association with underlying social factors. A link exists between D.S.H. and long-term unemployment with a prevalence nearly more than ten times higher in men (Platt, S. and Kreitman, 1984:161). Similarly with marital status, in Oxford particularly high rates were found in teenage wives, single and divorced women aged 24-35 years and in single men aged 30-40 years. The occurrence of D.S.H. in married subjects being far more common where there had been recent separation (Bancroft et.al., 1975: 170-177).

(b) Assessment of Risk

This is a difficult task, however, there are a number of 'prediction of intent/risk scales' that may be useful for clergy and laity in their initial interviews with those at risk. A simple list devised by Burglass, D. and Horton (1974:573-8) has proved fairly reliable in predicting whether those who have committed D.S.H. will be a short-term risk of a further attempt: The following six characteristics are examined to see if they are present -

1. Sociopathy - poor social circumstances and relationships
2. Alcohol/drug abuse
3. Any previous inpatient psychiatric treatment
4. Any previous outpatient psychiatric treatment
5. Previous D.S.H. resulting in hospital admission
6. Not living with a relative.

All carers, whilst initially concerned with establishing a sensitive rapport with an individual, will nevertheless want to establish, if possible, to what degree there is strong evidence of suicidal intent. Following the pioneer work of Tuckman and Youngman (1968:17-19) Beck et.al. (1974b) has developed a *Suicidal Intent Scale* (See Appendix 3) that I have used in presenting cases that provided insight. It deals with circumstances surrounding the attempt and the individual's feelings at the time, high scores denoting high suicidal intent. The scale is easy to administer and can be incorporated into the first or second interview.

Taken in isolation, intent scores can be only of limited value, but together with careful evaluation of the individual's problems, family background and coping resources, they may provide perspective. Once again it was found that such a scale was more closely associated with feelings of hopelessness than with depression. (Wetzel, 1976:1069-73). The Beck *Hopelessness Scale* is commonly used today by professional therapists (Beck et. al., 1974b,861:5)

Because laity and clergy are likely to be unfamiliar with this form of appraisal I believe it will, in the long run, be necessary to provide resources and support from experienced practitioners, to those who meet the at-risk individual in their parochial setting. The individual carer, at the very least, can be the first agency of education when encountering a potential suicide, therefore, even for subsequent referring, a fairly organised approach is required.

In the first instance note should be taken of appearance, body language and the content of speech, all of which may indicate the presence of abnormal distress.   Deterioration in self-care is often associated with deterioration in self-image and should not be ignored. Evidence of tension, fears and dejection can be conveyed merely by the way people walk or sit. Speech that is negative in attitude to the future, distinguished by a general lack of concern for things/people normally considered important, are all primary clues. This is where factual, local knowledge can provide a wealth of insight.

A profile of risk might include the following information, a surprising amount of which can be garnered from a conversational but concerned style of interview.

1	Family background	Deprivation in childhood, broken family history, lack of contact or support.
2.	Personality	Antisocial, aggressive and impulsive behaviour, difficulties in personal relationships, vulnerable, criminal record.
3.	Psychiatric Symptoms	Anxiety, stress, depression, any previous treatment, current symptoms - schizoid or bizarre behaviour - need to refer immediately.
4.	Physical Illness	Chronic Pain, terminal illness, insomnia, epilepsy, drug and alcohol abuse.
5.	Previous Suicide Attempts	Number and circumstances of each incident, degree of intent, outcome.
6.	Current Problems	Unemployment, finance, isolation, bereavement, loneliness, self contempt.

(c) Hierarchy of Risk

Having decided that an element of risk exists it is important to try and establish to what degree. A useful method described by Dyre et. al. (1973:171-4) is to share the evaluation of risk with the individual, to relieve to some extent the burden of responsibility of the carer, since the individual is probably the best judge of how strong the urge is to end life. By asking them whether they can honestly make the following statement: 'no matter what happens I will not kill myself, accidentally or on purpose, at any time' Dyre and his colleagues believe that lack of such assurance may suggest the element of risk that is present.

A more comprehensive exploration is contained in a model by Vaughan (1984:14-16) which uses a 'step towards suicide' process, each step representing a distinct stage of risk. The first four steps are considered more as examples of 'cries for help' whilst the final two steps appear to be directly motivated by a desire to relieve crippling despair.

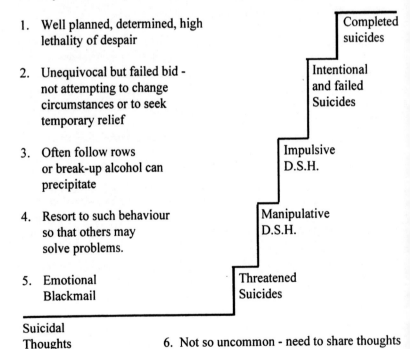

1. Well planned, determined, high lethality of despair — Completed suicides

2. Unequivocal but failed bid - not attempting to change circumstances or to seek temporary relief — Intentional and failed Suicides

3. Often follow rows or break-up alcohol can precipitate — Impulsive D.S.H.

4. Resort to such behaviour so that others may solve problems. — Manipulative D.S.H.

5. Emotional Blackmail — Threatened Suicides

Suicidal Thoughts

6. Not so uncommon - need to share thoughts

It is important to remember in the above model that each category of intent is subject to a whole range of risk factors - some as the result of underlying society-induced stress and others as a result of early psychodynamic impairment. Also, the individual may not be conscious of what they intend to do at any one time or in which direction they feel they are being driven. Alcohol, trauma, loss, etc. may then become the 'triggers' that determine the step which is taken.

Carers meet individuals at different stages of risk and therefore any intervention will need to take this fact into account. For example, those indicating suicidal thinking or fantasising where there is evidence of social or inter-personal problems may be only slightly at risk. Help may be given in enabling individuals to talk about such problems, putting them into perspective, planning the medium term and liaising with other professions.

Medium risk may highlight the presence of bereavement, isolation, deep feelings of worthlessness, depression and abuse of alcohol. Therefore, frequent, close supervision and befriending may be applicable. Counselling, some exploration of psychiatric symptoms and attempts to resolve social or personal problems may all be helpful. Where the signs are made much more concrete - open declaration of intent and indications of planning, then the risk begins to look dangerously imminent. The removal of potential dangers, consideration of hospital support and continual monitoring may be urgently required.

(d) Attitudes towards D.S.H.

It is important to remember that the demarcation line between suicide and D.S.H. is by no means a clear one. There exists a significant over-lap group which consists of those with long-term psychological instability and multiple social problems, together with those with no history of previous attempts but who are handicapped by immature psychodynamic development. Both groups are unable to deal adequately with adverse life events and both may be prompted to self destructive behaviour by social catastrophe. Since 30-40% of those who eventually kill themselves have a history of D.S.H. (Barraclough et.al., 1974:355) it will be crucial therefore that approaches are collectively informed and multi-disciplined.

Clearly, the medical attitude will affect the sort of in/out patient care that is on offer. However, it will also influence the attitudes of all other carers, who may well determine their responses to behaviour by perceived diagnoses. Those who are presented with the confidences of an individual need to help explore what problems may have caused an attempt and what are the sincere intentions of the person.

Needless to say, normative judgement is to be avoided especially where, with the individual's permission, other perspectives as to motivation are canvassed from interested parties. An important finding reveals that the general population more often regard D.S.H. as a phenomenon that happens to a person, rather than events that the person intentionally brings about. (Ginsberg, 1971:200)

Above all, the autonomy and freedom of individuals under extreme stress who react with such behaviour must be respected and faced together. Deliberate self-harm may then be seen as extreme reaction to extreme circumstances by individuals who so often are ill-equipped to cope at that moment.

3. Suicide and the Family – The Social Systemic Context

Of late there has been an encouraging movement away from a narrow focus on the individual exhibiting suicidal behaviour, who is so often seen as the deviant, to a broader examination of the family in which distress occurs. Forefront in this work is David Aldridge's detailed enquiry into the social systemic context of suicide (Aldridge, 1998) and in this section I am heavily indebted to Professor Aldridge for the insights he has provided.

Though there has been considerable research into the phenomenon of suicidal behaviour, it still remains unclear how, in process terms, the links between social factors and distress management within the family contribute to the final outcome. Aldridge concludes that 'behaviour is not understood when it is isolated from social systemic contexts' (page 11) indeed, though suicide can appear 'impulsive' it is often socially related in nature. Suicide and destructive self-harm can be seen in one sense, therefore, as symptomatic and one result of dangerous levels in family distress.

It is apparent (see chapter 2) that major disruptions in key relationships (work, school, college, personal and family) are crucial in suicidal behaviour (Gupta, Sivakumar and Smeeton, 1995; Kienhorst et al., 1995; Young, 1994) similarly with those isolated from families and networks of significant others, a significant factor with middle-aged male suicides (Heikkinen t al., 1995). With this in mind, it will be important for clergy and pastoral workers at parish level to help uncover the reasons for both personal isolation and family disharmony in their support work, drawing upon the latest guidance of psycho-social evidence.

Because major changes in family contexts are significant contributors to distress and anxiety (such as major rifts between individuals, illness in the family, children leaving home and changes in social status in the household) such local knowledge, though of a 'sensitive' nature, is of great value in exploring family tensions and circumstances and in developing a mutually agreed care programme.

Although the Church is anxious to pray for the sick and play its part in supporting families, it must be remembered that in the West, being labelled a 'sick' person, for whatever reason, can be difficult for some to accept. Referral itself, particularly for psychological help can be perceived as socially stigmatising, especially if there are no clear physical symptoms.

The Church needs to be more understanding of 'hidden' distress whilst ministering to the whole family situation.   It is too easy to blame the individual alone who presents the very symptoms that signal either collapse or inappropriate distress management. 'Knowing' and supporting families at parish level is therefore more than merely being neighbourly or caring in some general sense for individuals.

Being aware of social stressors peculiar to the situation and the signs of escalating distress, means being in touch at all levels with the family. The kindness of friends and neighbours is very important, all the more so if it means offering an unrestricted time and opportunity to talk through what is happening.

What Aldridge is suggesting, I believe, is that the social meaning of suicidal behaviour from the perspective of close and extended family networks, is an understanding to which a number of agencies can contribute and complement.   Interestingly, there appears to be only a limited amount of research on how the individual and the family perceive what is happening to them, together with the narration of their findings using the language of the particular family.   Simply 'medicalising' the problem, so often, is to focus solely on the symptomology of the 'deviant'.

Listening to the individual and the family as a whole is at the core of this therapeutic encounter, which all carers know to be a very labour-intensive and time-consuming process.   Because the professional is available only in a strictly limited and prescribed way, it could be argued that the caring friend or neighbour offers potentially a wider and more sustained, comprehensive support, especially where there is already in place training and supervision resources as an additional aid.

It is well-known that it is in the context of family difficulties that adolescent suicidal behaviour occurs (Kerfoot et al., 1996) Where there is lack of cohesion and internal family conflict, loss of emotional sustenance or meaningful relationships, families are prone to social stressors. This makes it even more urgent that the focus be directed toward the whole family rather than on the struggling individual.   Anything that will encourage, at least to some degree, family discourse, trusting and sharing, in this respect is of value.

In this respect, how the Church responds to unemployment, divorce, major illness and movement within families is crucial, both in its open debate at society level and in its action and initiatives with troubled families and individuals.   Of course, besides reaching out practically to those in special need is the desire to welcome sufferers to our centres of care and this means the provision of facilities to encourage accessibility.

The development and maintenance of fringe clubs, drop-in centres for the young, mums and toddlers groups, cosy clubs for the aged and infirm are therefore more important than we might imagine in offering places and situations conducive to talking and sharing, making 'asking for help' more acceptable and less the result of 'failing'.

In general terms, encouraging church members and allied pastoral caring agencies to talk more openly about self-harm, depression and 'feeling trapped' and in very simple ways working to remove obstacles which may prevent vulnerable people seeking support, is more than merely a worthy cause but rather a realisation of the Christian commission to heal.

Similarly, opening up discussion in church, college chapel and school assembly can also help challenge the taboo of self-harm.   Also, raising awareness of the pernicious results of stress in the work place and in education, both for those who teach and those who study and supporting overtly organisations that minister to 'at risk' individuals and groups (the homeless, young men, prisoners, those in high risk occupations) can also assist the skilling of carers to this vital work.

Without, in any way, suggesting a prying attitude to family concerns, ministers should be aware, nevertheless, that family histories can furnish compelling clues as to how destructive behaviour develops.   For in such families there is often a 'family culture of distress management' that includes confrontation, denial, threat and even blackmail and where medication and abuse of food, drugs and alcohol contribute to suicide, self-harm and sometimes murder.

Such histories can reveal an escalation of dysfunctional behaviour over a number of generations and it is well-known (Koopmans, 1995; Martin et al., 1995) that children with one or more family members who have died by their own hand, are at more risk of attempting suicide than children who do not have such a family history. (Guiterrez, King and Ghaziuddin, 1996)

In short, Aldridge states that 'distress is managed as it is manifested, how distress can be expressed is also learned' (page 48), i.e. some suicidal behaviours are attempts to resolve distress by control and modification of family environment. Helping families to recognise the way in which they currently handle distress can be an important contribution to changes of behaviour.

We all, as we develop individually, have to learn ways of dealing with change. Families too have to find positive ways of accommodating such change, preferably without excessive levels of hostility or conflict. It seems clear that distress for some families is managed by one family member exhibiting symptoms. They fast become the 'scapegoat' or token deviant and such a circular pattern of hostility and distrust is difficult to break since the threat of suicidal behaviour can itself be a significant part of a family's pattern of communication.

To help minister to such families is to listen and respond to the stories that people themselves tell to make sense of their own lives and the quandary they find themselves in. In discovering what the individual means, we may detect the influences specific to any particular family that affect thinking and also indicate that point at which families have exhausted their own psychological and emotional resources.

'From a family systems theory approach, persons who interact together regularly relate in an organised manner' (Reiss, 1981) i.e. in any family relationship there can be detected a pattern associated with its ability to change. But where behaviour must obey fixed and inflexible rules some problem behaviour may be seen as a cry for help or a pathetic attempt to change family practices.

Instead of focusing on the individual (usually held to be responsible for his own behaviour) we might instead work at the form and broader narrative of a family's language. It is well known that many suicide attempters contact a helping agency during the week(s) prior to the attempt (Bancroft et al., 1977; Birtchnell, 1973) these attempters say that they needed someone primarily 'to talk to'. Aldridge states that a 'medical practitioner, as a agent of primary care delivery, is often chosen, although it could be a priest or a social worker depending upon how the distress itself is construed'.

Most workers in the field are aware of certain characteristics that are significant in families that experience an attempted suicide. They include: social isolation, unemployment, divorce and a whole mix of social problems. As a church we can and we must push locally to improve poor housing and isolation, but it is also important to see how people see themselves and if their beliefs are located in psycho-social explanations relating to stress and unemployment, etc.

I believe, that these are the sorts of problems that other listening bodies can attend to, GP's are not necessarily the appropriate people to help where such causes are identified. Researchers, notably, are known to focus on those characteristics which are amenable to description and examination but others, including the Church, can help uncover other sometimes more dense and diffuse problems concerning re-marriage, sibling rivalry, bereavement and major change.

The need to talk about death and dying, sexual orientation, parents relinquishing their hold on growing teenagers are all important matters which can give rise to situations of emergency. Whilst these are being attended to, the support of friends and carers (especially following disastrous negative confrontations) can be significant in recovery for individual and family. Without such intervention, is it so surprising that sometimes the most vulnerable and least able individual in the family, simply does 'not want to be there anymore' and 'can't cope' so commencing an overdose habitual strategy that may be repeated at subsequent times of distress.

So often, suicide attempters regard their distress as being theirs alone and 'personal' i.e. 'no-one understands'. What is needed is objective listening that can also embrace referral to practical supports: financial and social. Most of all, they may desire someone to 'believe them' and legitimate their view of themselves. Professional social workers and counsellors are not always best placed to arrive on the doorstep unheralded for a chat or a cup of tea, walk in the park or whatever.

True friendship, I believe, can be both personal and objective involving as it does unconditional acceptance and empathy. After all, as friends or even as acquaintances, we are not there to 'treat' them, we are befriending and this is an active role which, though limited, does not rob the individual of autonomy but values them as human beings (even the Samaritans have such limitations to contend with).

Sharing a meal, shopping, etc. though mundane are activities which can literally be a life-line to a vulnerable person which allows their emergent 'self' to be seen without undue pressure. Though they cannot go it alone, yet together with the other, we can help strengthen an approach to living which entails shared understanding of 'meaning' and encourages the verbalisation of compelling, negative thoughts and dark fears.

Through befriending the need to tease out frustrations and self-destructive thoughts is more likely to be achieved in a much less threatening atmosphere. We must take individuals seriously and their family context, listening to their suggestions for the future and attempting to incorporate them. This is not only caring but healing by engagement with the other through a therapeutic dialogue.

While such work is taking shape, clergy and laity carers can also help the monitoring of circumstances, working, if professionals are agreeable, with the co-operation of GP's social workers and other agencies. Helping may mean interacting and identifying with all significant others, noting what is currently happening and what had happened before. We will need to attend to:

1. Description of presenting problem and its behavioural nature within the context of the family.
2. What concretely is happening now.
3. Significant intersectional features.
4. The recurring problem. What had happened before?
5. Gaining permission to share in a concerted team approach of support.
6. Since suicide attempts are about 'feeling', this needs to be ascertained as fully as possible and replayed to the individual and family (to understand how they see the world).
7. Gauge suicidal intent if possible, using a suitable instrument of enquiry.
8. Note signs of change – is it possible to help them to make sense of their lives.
9. Support after any hospitalisation is vital (it is known that where there is no significant movement in improved circumstances then there can be a high repetition rate within three months of discharge after an overdose: Hawton and Catalan, 1982; Runeson, Eklund and Wasserman, 1996).
10. Help plan a more positive future.

Too often, repetition in an individual is seen merely as evidence of their intractable problem rather than an indication that the family context remains unchanged. Though we may not be the persons who help to bring about specific or definitive change for individuals or families, we can nevertheless be part of that process. Where GP's are primarily concerned with personal health, physical or mental, there will always be a tendency to ignore the contextual nature of presenting problems. As befriending Christians we can help address this situation by our willingness to interact within the social systemic context.

4. Suicide and the Young Person

'The stark reality is that suicide is the second most common cause of death amongst young people, taking more lives than cancer', so writes Simon Armson (Samaritan's Chief Executive, May 1997, 'Exploring the Taboo'). With this reality in mind and before examining a case illustration drawn from the Witney Deanery Survey, that points up graphically the characteristic suffering of the young person, let us reflect upon the facts.

From the ages of 12 to 25 years the child gradually becomes the adult via a sometimes painful process of development (especially in adolescence). There is not only rapid physical and mental growth but also intellectual and emotional development that makes for a sometimes difficult birth into a personal identity and growing independence.

This development can be a period of highly charged rebellion, for autonomy requires separation from parents and with this a sensitive process of dis-engagement by guardians and carers. Today, puberty starts early with young people craving for emotional maturity and parents at a loss to understand fully what is happening. To complicate matters, boys and girls reveal and cope with the ensuing emotional distress in quite different ways.

Boys that are struggling may well show their pain by behaving badly; fighting, truanting and stealing, the aggression serving to provide an outlet for pent-up emotion. Girls, on the other hand, may be more likely to suppress their anger, though this can precipitate depression (twice as common amongst women as men – Weissman and Klerman, 1977).

As they grow older, young men are not only reluctant to define their problems as emotional ones, but are less inclined to look for professional help. Also their coping strategies may gradually become less effective which may mean a heavier reliance on alcohol and drugs to relieve their anxiety and sometimes depression.

Though, on balance, young women appear more socialised in viewing themselves and their problems, when stressed they are more likely, because of their often distaste for violence, to self-poison. Of particular concern has been the comparatively high suicide rate of 16-24 year old women of Asian origin than among those of British origin. Similarly with young Black women, the causes are thought to be connected with racism, family conflicts and fears of a hostile living environment.

Though society seems more tolerant of minority groups, nevertheless gay, lesbian and bi-sexual youth are driven to self destruction. The London Gay Teenage Project in 1984 reported that one in five of the mainly male teenagers in its study had attempted suicide because of their sexuality.

As we have seen (Chapter 2), young people in prison and remand centres are at a dangerously high risk of suicide, often through stress, isolation, intimidation and the length of their sentence. Loss of family and loved ones and paradoxically abuse within families, amounts for a significant number of young suicide attempts. Nearly 60% of victims in one British study were abused by family members (Mrazel et al., 1993).

Though young people may display difficult behaviour such as aggression and recklessness, deep unhappiness is still just as likely to result in depression, anxiety, eating disorders and even phobias. At least four out of ten young people who kill themselves had shown signs of severe depression beforehand in a study in 1993 (Martunnen et al.) Though there is a relatively small incidence of major mental problems amongst the young, nevertheless schizophrenic symptoms usually appear between the ages of 17 and 25 years of age.

The young, like older adults, to relieve intolerable tension and emotional pain, will take refuge in alcohol and drugs, indeed alcohol abuse in general is associated with depression, anxiety and other mental health problems (Gelder et al. 1989) It seems clear that such substances may be used as a strategy for maintaining control or block out panic when a young persons fears disintegration.

Apart from study or employment problems, relationships with partners or family are the most often mentioned problems of young suicide attempters. But since the 1960's there has been an enormous slackening of restrictions to far as sexual licence is concerned with premarital sex becoming increasingly common amongst 14 and 15 year olds. Which means many more intense, short-term and highly charged sexual liasons, which when they go wrong can cause enormous and profound pain.

It has been suggested that with young people, certainly in school situations, there may be insight to be gained from looking at developments in the USA. There was a 300% rise in teenage suicides in the USA between 1960 and 1980 and increasingly suicide prevention programmes are being initiated in school situation, the general aim being to raise awareness and encourage vulnerable youngsters to seek appropriate help. With this in mind, I wish to turn now to a particular case with which I am familiar and then to look at how best to begin raising awareness in a school setting.

5. Education - A key to prevention?

Parents of the case illustration that follows, when interviewed, were unaware of the problems that Michael had been suffering at the time of the crisis. They had noticed signs of disturbance but like most parents confused it with the onset of puberty. In retrospect they realised that communication itself had been the central weakness in their ability to influence and support their son. This had not been conveyed to those in loco parentis and so, like thousands of teenagers, their son was at risk, not so much because of the particular crisis but because of the lack of accessible support. Many young people find it difficult to confide in those who are closest to them, particularly when they are going through the inevitable separation process of youth.

The case illustration that follows is by no means untypical and together with analysis I trust the reader will see that a Christian response can be both pragmatic and educative providing carers are aware that (a) there exists a genuine and widespread problem of suffering amongst the young that can provoke D.S.H.; (b) this is not simply a 'medical problem', and (c) that school and church can encourage saving initiatives at these crucial points in children's development. Christianity, through the model of the Good Shepherd, extends to the young and the most vulnerable in society, concern, understanding and forgiveness, it is for us to formulate how best to mobilise our human resources to channel this care in society.

Case Illustration - Michael (6d)

Michael, a thirteen year old adolescent, some years earlier and in a previous boarding school, had been seriously molested over a protracted period by a fellow pupil. This traumatic experience of sexual bullying had gone undetected by parents and staff, and though he had attended a couple of counselling session at the time, the effects were to lead to near fatal consequences in 1993.

Michael, an attractive and bright boy, during the first term of his new school had become not only unhappy and anxious but uncharacteristically scruffy. Though he had gone through a miserable patch some years earlier, his parents did not consider that further counselling was needed. They preferred to put his extreme behaviour down to the typical unsettled emotions of galloping puberty. As time went on, however, the degree of his responses to his new situation appeared more and more extreme.

Educationally, he was not flourishing nor was he mixing with his peers, as his House Master put it, he was behaving 'like a puppy that couldn't settle.' Accustomed to boarding school life, he had become a loner, finding it impossible to share his problems with anyone.

The school noticed his strained and haggard appearance but took no steps to ascertain the reasons, the tutorial/pastoral system not being as efficient and sensitive as it might have been. Michael felt 'mixed-up' and was beginning to cause alarm by boasting that he had taken drugs/alcohol and now considered himself a homosexual!

Nor was he sleeping well, appearing dreamy, disconnected and lacking concentration. He began to be quite agitated, flying into tantrums and bouts of incessant arguing. His behaviour was considered no more than 'attention seeking', but there was more to his condition than anyone realised.

He confessed later that he felt a need to be with older boys to whom he was able to confide that 'something had happened to him, a long time ago.' He felt that he would not have peace of mind until his parents knew what had happened to him, but he felt unable to find the courage to tell them, considering that they would probably be shocked and unsympathetic.

Eventually, and quite fortuitously his House Master picked up this information third-hand and advised Michael that no one in the school would help him until he himself plucked up the courage to confront his parents. Michael began to feel increasingly tense and isolated as in his mind, the problem grew to huge proportions.

Very soon an opportunity arose at which Michael proposed to broach the subject of his long-standing shame and guilt. However, he failed to do this and was unable to persuade his House Master to come to his rescue. As a result he felt annoyed with himself, frustrated and deeply troubled. That evening, feeling desperate, he swallowed some drugs prescribed for a minor ailment that he knew, nevertheless, taken in excess could have serious side effects. Next morning, feeling unwell, he was taken to hospital and his problem, much to his relief, was officially brought to the notice of his parents.

(a) Recognising Adolescents at Risk from Crisis

With young adolescents a crisis that can provoke self-harm does not develop instantaneously, there are identifiable interacting stages of development, albeit over a relatively short period of time, that lead to active crisis. These stages are psychological in character and vary somewhat depending on the kind of traumatic event being experienced. By recognising these phases and intervening, carers can help prevent a stressful life event from becoming a full-blown crisis.

PHASE 1

Events like Michael's now school with all the difficulties of settling, the onset of puberty, the unconscious fear of further bullying, the desire to disabuse himself of his shameful secret, causes an **initial rise in anxiety** which sets in order a series of reactions that culminate in a crisis. However, any one of those contributory factors does not in itself constitute a crisis. Rather, it is Michael's inability to cope, his vulnerability through unresolved long-term trauma and his displaced anger and frustration with his parents, graphically displayed in an over reaction to his peers and compensation through bravado, that finally provokes self-destructive behaviour.

Adolescents usually respond to difficult, painful or potentially traumatic events with familiar problem-solving mechanisms to reduce the stress and discomfort arising from excessive anxiety. Michael cannot face it and as he has a tendency to be a loner, he finds it difficult to ask for help. Instead he displays acts of bravado to disguise the pain.

PHASE 2

For a number of years he had felt that it would be better if he could keep his secret to himself, but this knowledge gnaws away at him resulting in bizarre angry over-reactions to adverse circumstances. In this second phase his **usual problem-solving ability fails** while the stimulus (boarding again with potentially intimidating peers) causing the initial rise in anxiety, continues.

Michael grows more despondent and more isolated and anxious. In interview he says that he wanted to assert himself and tell his guilty secret to his parents, knowing that this would get rid of his pain 'once and for all' however, he was already considering that there might only be one way out. Michael badly wanted his parents' approval and sympathy, but in this uncontrollable situation the possibility of acute crisis increased. This was by no means inevitable, the school being willing to help but only on condition that he made the first move to confide in his parents.

PHASE 3

Michael's anxiety level rises further and the increased tension moves him to use every resource available. He needs to attract attention to himself so that others may discover his problems, since he cannot divulge them directly. He says he has taken drugs (against school rules) that he might be homosexual and he becomes strangely depersonalised and 'dreamy', lack of sleep affecting his overall health.

His parents, sensing that all was not well, visited him. But in their meeting together he reverted to form, and much to the annoyance of his House Master was unable to raise the issue. His problem-solving opportunity missed, and feeling exhausted, he is in full-blown crisis.

PHASE 4

The final phase is that of a **state of active crisis** that results when (i) internal strength and social support are lacking or the person is unable to fully utilise existing support (ii) the person's personal problem remains unresolved (iii) tension and anxiety rise to an unbearable degree. Michael responds to his predicament by impulsively swallowing tablets when in a state of frustration and near exhaustion. Afterwards he said he did not want to die but he did not know what to do, he wanted others to solve his problem.

This case, I believe, illustrates several important points about the crisis experience, for although he is a normal adolescent, Michael was at risk on several counts. First, he faces the developmental challenge of achieving adult independence, secondly, he wants to erase the past unfortunate experiences and assert himself regarding his future, however, he has the simultaneous challenge of relating to a new school environment with unfamiliar peers. Meeting these challenges with the ever present sense of stigma from his previous experience, would have been easier if at first he had not been so reluctant to ask for help and he had felt that he could confide fully in his parents.

However, both staff and parents did not interpret signs of stress because they were largely disguised by similar symptoms of the onset of puberty. If they had, they might have arranged a meeting with parents and staff present or negotiated another course of action if Michael's attempt to divulge had failed. Leaving him with the full burden and no pastoral input led to a dangerous crisis.

This case also reveals that suicidal responses to traumatic life events most often do not occur in places where mental health specialists are immediately available, hence the importance of front-line carers (best friend, school matron, chaplain or teacher) and the need to be vigilant to early signs of stress and anxiety.

(b) Centrality of Communication in Successful Crisis Intervention

As we have seen, Michael's fundamental problem was one of communicating the full extent of his long-lasting problem to a significant other person. One of the tactics that distinguishes crisis intervention from some traditional psychotherapy processes is the directive action of a would be carer. A sensitive teacher, chaplain, matron, will need to pay special attention to the loner and to the depressed, because a prominent characteristic of their behaviour is their reluctance or inability to ask for help.

Ideally, the carer needs to positively **reach out** to the distressed in a protective way i.e. seeking out, expressing concern, listening and in general, creating an atmosphere and opportunity for confidences to be shared. All of which is going to be easier and more fruitful if good rapport already exists between students and staff, where student's needs are anticipated and where carers take the leading role in initiating communication.

Such communication is unlikely however, for those who still harbour the myth that talking about self destruction with people suspected of being suicidal, will inevitably put the idea into their heads. Clinical experience and research reveals that nothing could be further from the truth. The process of deciding to commit suicide is much more complicated than that.

A person who is not already suicidal will not become so by a direct question from someone intending to help - indeed they are very often relieved when someone is sensitive enough to respond to their despair and thus help protect them from themselves. Sharing the terrifying feelings of suicidal impulses becomes possible only when empathic support is conveyed, thus lessening the need to 'act out' troubled feelings.

Persistence in this common myth about suicide serves a purpose, as all myths do. In general it prevents one from having to confront the fearful prospect that another feels suicidal, and with it the need to take action unilaterally. Hence, by not responding, one is relieved of any responsibility. Nothing is more important in crisis intervention than direct communication, only in this way can one assess the degree of suicidal risk.

Adolescents like Michael, even though he is bright, talented and without a history of psychological illness or behavioural problems, are vulnerable to further crisis episodes. They may well benefit from counselling to enable them to gain insight into their vulnerability, and become familiar with more healthy coping strategies. As a general rule it is considered that follow-up care is indicated for anyone who responds to a life crisis with a suicide attempt. This highlights the potential learning aspects of crisis, a less than healthy response to a stressful situation can be educative providing there is opportunity and space for reflection. Individuals need to be helped to view their lives from a different perspective and this requires the objective care and unconditional acceptance of another.

(c) Raising Awareness in a School Setting

It appears that nation-wide, no hard data exists concerning the incidence of reported D.S.H. amongst young people in state or independent schools, nor is there any comprehensive policy or standardised policy of report or referral. It seems that many cases are either covered-up or referred privately.

In the case of Michael, though the school's pastoral system was faulty, they had developed a system of instant referral to the local city hospital where health specialists combined with social services were able to assess his situation and arrange for further consultations. Subsequent counselling was purchased through the local GP practice since free treatment was not available at county level.

Until data is available it remains impossible to establish the true extent of the problem, however, in view of recent estimates, a valuable short-term objective would be to research perceived need and to explore the role of teaching staff in identifying and actively responding to the vulnerable. To do this there will need to be wider dissemination of information and understanding of D.S.H. to achieve a greater awareness of risk especially connected to bullying in schools.

It is my belief that in this way, schools will then be in a better and more informed position to make major contributions to:

    (i)   Prevention - developing strategies to ameliorate the condition that can lead some to self destructive behaviour.

    (ii) Intervention - treatment and care of suicidal crises.

(iii) Postvention (Schneidman, 1974) - dealing with the traumatic after effects in survivors, i.e. children, parents and teachers.

It is not widely recognised, in spite of the continued rise in D.S.H. in the young, that schools may well provide a logical forum for the integration of intervention efforts, students are in a school setting for seven hours a day and for up to two-thirds of the year. School personnel interact daily with the young, have the opportunity to observe their changes in behaviour (more uninhibited than at home) and can understand the stressful situations they encounter, so responding to direct or subtle cries for help.

Such exploration may well reveal important opportunities to both predict and avert self-destructive behaviour. It also seems clear that if those at risk were fully determined to die there would be few warning signs and fewer non-lethal attempts, however, this is not the case. Indeed, it has been estimated that inner conflicts are communicated, all too often, through verbal statements and observable behaviour changes by 80% of those at risk (Smith, 1986).

The question of why such responsibilities for recognising warning signs might be devolved in some measure to schools may be justified on the following grounds. That schools, providing they enjoy the full confidence and co-operation of parents, have not only a responsibility to help students develop into productive citizens who can contribute positively to society, but are able to identify and resolve problems that interfere with the educational process.

As professionals they will be experienced and familiar with students of particular age groups and most of the problems that beset the adolescent. As part of the wider brief of education, a variety of staff representing a number of disciplines working within a caring pastoral system, ought to be able to read the signs that can be missed by parents whose children are actively involved in the natural process of disengagement from them.

As has become apparent in Chapter 2, there are always underlying contributory factors at work and there is some evidence to suggest that the relative affluence of Britain may itself be significant. Lester (1988:955) has shown that nations with a high quality of life have higher suicide rates and he explains this phenomenon by referring to an earlier theory proposed by Hendry, A.F. and Short (1954) who argued that when people have a clear external source to blame for their misfortune, they are more likely to be angry and less likely to be suicidal. In which case it might be argued that a relatively high quality of life, as enjoyed by the majority of youth today, means fewer external events to blame one's misery on, and so D.S.H. may become more common.

So therefore, though critics complain that the young have 'never had it so good', their need remains. A school-inspired programme of D.S.H.. awareness would be familiar with the affluent sub-culture in which most students reside and may well be best-placed to meet anxiety and stress with strategies that reinforce the need for a more positive self-concept in the young.

To begin with, whilst accurate data is being collated, it would be prudent to develop, on a pilot basis, such a D.S.H. awareness initiative, carefully evaluating its findings and methods, before co-ordinating an area or county task force or advisory council. This could be made up of Community Health, School, Social Services, Samaritans and Church representatives, all of whom can be instrumental in establishing a structure of support, that provides not merely a 'safety net' for the vulnerable, but is committed to nurturing a confidential and trusting relationship with youngsters.

Each individual or community school-based initiative might include the following developmental steps:

(i)   Initial needs assessment conducted to establish the extent of D.S.H. in school situations.
(ii) Raising awareness by conveying accurate information both to schools, children and parents.
(iii) Enabling a more open process of sharing of experience so as to establish a network of support amongst parents, schools and community-based organisations.
(iv) Explore fully the need for a clear policy regarding observations, reporting, response and intervention.
(v)   Plan individual programmes complete with short and long-term goals.
(vi) Establish on-going training for teachers and all involved in counselling, evaluate programme by providing continual monitoring to include data collection.

(d) Fostering Positive self-concept in Youth

It is thought that the most effective way of preventing D.S.H. amongst the young is to aim to provide each child with an upbringing and education that is conducive to the development of a positive self-concept. Roughly defined this is the way a person feels about themselves, if you wish, the image of self that exists in their own minds. It embraces both self-acceptance, what Christianity sees as valuing oneself regardless of perceived weakness, and self-esteem i.e. feeling good about one's self on the basis of perceived strengths.

Such a self concept is composed of four interrelated and interactive components, and these are recognised by most caring counsellors (Long, V.O., 1987:15-17) (i) **Competency**, the development of skills and abilities which allow individuals to take charge of their lives, work, relationships and self which, together with (ii) **Self-esteem**, that makes for a better sense of self regulation and confidence (ii) **Congruency** - that ability and pride in being oneself, balanced with (iv) **Self-control** that should make for greater self responsibility and self-approval. Promoting a self-concept then will mean fostering both self-esteem and self-acceptance.

It is now thought that suicide crisis intervention, in the past, may have been unsuccessful because the efforts were directed only at the symptoms rather than close examination of the initial problem and its family context. It is known that suicide is a multi-causal phenomenon and it is likely therefore that risk factors, when traced back, will reveal failure to develop a positive self-concept, which is critical to the survival of youth.

Mounting research shows that the full-functioning child is very different from the person who flounders through life displaying a poorly-developed sense of self (Briggs, 1970:3). Educational psychologist Erik Erikson believes that to achieve adequate self-esteem requires the resolution of three basic tensions during early childhood: (i) trust verses mistrust (ii) autonomy verses doubt and (iii) initiative verses guilt. (See Case Illustration - Renton). These tensions should be seen as sequential, resolution of one preparing the way for the next.

The earlier these tensions are addressed and resolved the more equipped the child will be in coping with recurring problems. Early self-esteem development (the way the child judges himself) affects not merely problem solving (Michael's case) but also influences his creativity, integrity and stability. There is convincing evidence that points to a relation between self-esteem and academic success, drug abuse, pre-marital intercourse, running away and adolescent deviant activity (Leonardson, 1986: 467; Erikson et. al., 1986:501)

When the young are not successful in attaining and maintaining high self esteem, they may erect defences. In Michael's case they were primarily sublimation: boasting of having taken drugs, attempting a new persona as a homosexual, and denial: separation from the stressful situation as a 'loner'. Like adults, adolescents with an impaired self-image may come to depend on external signs of their work. This is dangerous because any failure in work or relationships can precipitate D.S.H. (Hafen, B.W. and Fransden, 1986)

Psychological abuse, intended or not, is significantly high in families of the suicidal (Holden, 1984:839) particularly where there have been difficulties in early parent/child relationships. Parents are, as in Renton's case, often frustrating, rejecting and even unkind, wanting the child's presence to a degree but unwilling to make a full emotional investment. The child may strive to fulfil his parents' expectations whilst deriving no pleasure in doing so, or, the child does not feel free to act in ways that would separate him from his parents. (Hendin, 1987:151)

Because children view themselves in the way they think their 'significant others' feel about them, then the responsibility to convey role models that encourage positive self-concept is vital, especially amongst parents, teachers, clergy and friends. This will mean treating the young with respect and expecting a reciprocal response: loving them unconditionally accepting strengths and weaknesses; legitimating them to express good and bad feelings without rejection and helping them to discover acceptable ways to behave in areas of difficulty.

We may begin with trying to project a living model as Christians of one's own self esteem, this may then be recognised by the young. In the school situation Briggs (1970) explores some useful building blocks of self-esteem development that a Christian way of life would want to emulate: reinforce positive life experiences; guard against the development of impossible demands on self; not merely accept the young but cherish them; encourage autonomy and personal responsibility whilst dealing non-judgementally with failure.

A basic rule about human behaviour is that negative feelings exist before negative acts. (Michael's example). If those feelings are allowed to be expressed and listened to in an empathic fashion, then negative behaviour can be prevented. My belief is, that 'poor coping' stems essentially from the impaired early development of individual self-regulating mechanisms essential in combating crisis and stress. Without them the adult may, many years later, be deprived of essential external supporting resources, and as a result be put at grave risk of self-injury.

Hence D.S.H. rather than being viewed as a medical disease, the main symptom being depression, might better be understood as an extreme response to a life which has become for that moment one of intolerable pain and distinguished by overwhelming feelings of hopelessness and helplessness. To understand this, the psychology of despair, is to better gauge an individual's intrinsic vulnerability so as to bring to bear strategies that are *essentially support-led.*

However, the individual will require more than practical support, for what lies at the centre of their distress is not only a lack of self-love but the *absence of an authentic love from without. A Christian response,* I believe, must seek therefore to utilise the shepherding qualities of a pastoral approach through the language and insight of the wounded healer. Such love, Christians believe, is a creative force, powerfully exemplified in the life of Christ, which in the hands of his followers can provide a potent instrument in meeting the human being's desire for wholeness.

CHAPTER FOUR

SUICIDE - A QUESTION OF SAVING INITIATIVES

1. The Theological Imperative

I began this enquiry into Christian responses to suicide by asserting that self-inflicted death is accepted by most people today, regrettably, as part of human living. I went on to say however, that where there is a conscientious effort to understand it, in the broadest terms, then Christians will be better enabled to meet the current crisis as a significant ministry of healing, and by so doing, able to learn at a deeper level more about the integrity and nature of their beliefs.

To help Christians understand suicide it is necessary to analyse carefully the external and internal causal relationships to be found in the human and physical factors of God's world. It seems clear that there is much ignorance associated with this issue, the Church concentrating on suicide as a question of Christian conscience to the virtual exclusion of the social and psychological sciences' contribution.

Theological reflection and action are concerned with asking how the transcendent God is being experienced within the lives of both victim and carer and also how Christians may respond in an overall enterprise of saving initiatives. Applying theology in this way serves as a vital tool in the transformation of God's work as a caring compassionate creation. For too long we have joined the mourners in the aftermath, offering sympathy and condolences, rather than applying our Christian resolve in meeting the suicide crisis with both practical and educative initiatives.

Thirty five years have passed since the Church of England published *Ought Suicide to be a Crime?* which anticipated changes in civil law in 1961, suicide ceasing to be a crime though those aiding and abetting could be prosecuted. In this document the moralists and the theologians struggled to find complete agreement on the degree of responsibility of individual cases. Also, though it was recognised that there might be various social and psychological causes for suicide the preoccupation remained still with the supposed 'cowards way out' and with the 'inadequate personalities' of the suicidal.

Suicide continued therefore to be recognised as sin though with exceptions (martyrdom and those which proceeded from 'mental derangement'). The first exception conformed with the accepted position of the

Church from Augustine onwards that only where there is a 'divine signal' in the calling to self sacrifice can voluntary death be tolerated, the second exception equating with the commonly held view that suicide is a 'medical problem'.

Apart from the arguments that (i) life is a gift that ought to be preserved (ii) suicide is a denial of self love by violating the sixth commandment, the third reason clearly regarded highly, was that life itself is a moral probation in which suffering and human struggles were recognised as disciplines. Today, the Church of England, having published no further guidance, the same position holds, that we are bidden to unite our sufferings with those of Christ and by so doing prove in them, the power of God displayed in the resurrection.

I would surmise, however, that only a proportion of any nation would have the spiritual fortitude to tolerate a miserable and painful life solely as an expression of faith, so what of the rest? If death is seen exclusively in terms of our last enemy (1Cor.15:26) an opportunity for the testing of the individual's faith, then we may conclude that our distinctive Christian attitude towards suicide arises primarily because of our rather partial attitude towards death. Voluntary death becomes purely a selfish act, a deliberate substitution of personal power for the power of Christ and hence a deliberate separating of the suicidal from God.

Because of a fundamental lack of understanding of the causal factors associated with suicide it continues to be depicted as faithless apostasy rather than human weakness. Similarly, though the Church recognises that those at risk ought to be 'speedily commended to the pastoral concern of the clergy' nevertheless there remains the assumption that the problem is one of a lack of moral and spiritual fibre. Similarly, clergy are to be 'offered more help in understanding this part of their pastoral duty' (1959:35) yet there have been no Archbishop or Synod inspired resources forthcoming. At a time when national statistics for suicide and D.S.H. remain alarmingly high this is to be deplored.

But what do other Churches have to say? Apart from a pastoral letter of note from the Archbishop of Cashel and Emly entitled *Suicide - A Permanent Solution to a Temporary Problem?* (1989) there has been little new guidance offered by the Roman Catholic Church. Commentary on the Commandments (catechism) continues to emphasise the preservation of life, since God is the owner and suicide is seen as an offence against the love of others and contrary to the will of God.

It does accept, however, that grave suffering can diminish a person's sense of responsibility, suggesting positive steps to ameliorate the social causes of despair. However, there is no clarion call for the Church to take a lead in championing greater recognition of the issue by a more proactive initiative.

The Methodist Church Department of Christian Citizenship in 1961, whilst noting that there were those who thought it wrong to relax traditional Christian condemnation of suicide, did accept that culpability was extremely precarious now that there was a greater scientific knowledge concerning the psychophysical factors involved. They conclude that the stigma attached to the act was probably more attributable to the attitudes of ecclesiastical authority rather than the law, and they welcomed further research into causal factors. However, a wide body of knowledge has been growing in the areas surveyed in this enquiry yet Church denominations seem not to have noted nor followed up these findings.

The General Assembly of the Church of Scotland in 1981 strongly confirmed their consistently held view that the Christian recognises no right to dispose of their own life, though those that do should be regarded with compassion and understanding rather than condemnation. Yet theological reflection still remains firmly rooted in ancient responses, rather than in renewed ministry to those at risk. Because churches tend to be isolated from collaborative efforts with other helping agencies, ignorant of the contributions of other disciplines and complacent in their almost total reliance on The Samaritans, their ministry fails to help meet the challenge.

In 1994 the General Assembly noted, significantly, that the public had become more accepting of suicide seeing it as tragedy rather than sin. I believe that as Christians we have not moved with new trends in thinking nor have we responded to need or engaged in critical debate, rather we continue to merely restate our position. It is time to put aside condemnation, it is for God alone to judge. Instead we must recognise that there cannot be positive and effective ministry without a genuine and authentic encounter by a Church that accepts its own pain and its own vulnerability as a valuable source of Christian outreach.

To do this, it will be important to understand the rich legacy of theological thought to be found in the writings of Augustine and Aquinas, but in an historical context and critically. Also, the theological imperative demands that we approach scripture with that sincere faith which seeks to rightly grasp God's self-disclosure, but always keeping in mind inherent ambiguities of thought.

In addition, if we believe that humanity's encounter with the Divine in Christ was in the context of history, then theology needs to continue to develop from today's cultural context in which a renewed ministry to the suicidal is best achieved by emulating the model of Christ himself, who acted inside situations and alongside people's experiences. Today, as a Church, we are not I fear, raising actively the issue nor are we responding effectively.

As we have seen, there are a number of factors to be considered in any explanation of suicide as a phenomenon, humankind being subject to both collective and individual forces of influence that are to be found in the many and varied situational triggers that make for 'poor coping'. These include financial, marital and relationship difficulties, unemployment, economic and political uncertainties, physical and cultural isolation, health and drug/alcohol related problems. From the profile it was apparent that vulnerable occupations such as medicine and agriculture attract clusters of triggers that raise the likelihood of suicide in those professions.

Any Christian initiative designed to combat the debilitating effects of unchecked situational pressures such as these will require accurate information on established need locally, wide dissemination of supporting resource materials and strategies put in place directed towards raising the issues. To make it a significant part of a pastoral responsibility will require the utilisation of existing skills and experience, so that it may form the focus of a healing ministry of the whole Church.

As can be seen from recent existing developments in Swansea Prison, a listening ministry remains at the centre of supporting initiatives to the helpless. Also, poor coping in prison has been seen to improve with the application of 'protecting agents' that are also applicable to the wider community: facilitating closer human contact, encouraging a constructive use of time, improving conditions of living and accommodation, above all, supporting individuals by enabling opportunities to talk with a meaningful other in a friendly and supportive environment.

If we believe as a Christian, in salvation, then we must include liberation, the releasing of the vulnerable in society, from crippling despair. Chapter Three of this enquiry has concerned itself with the specific development factors that conspire to make some human beings especially vulnerable to suicidal crisis. There are a number of theories, that vary in detail, but all agree that failure to develop at an early age self-regulating structures, in the main, results in inabilities to master anxiety and regulate self-esteem when under stressful conditions. This makes crucial the later acquisition of external compensatory supporting resources in the areas of relationship to others, work and self-parts. Where losses in any or all of these are sustained then the demand for substitute resources ('cries for help') will follow. Anticipating this at the earliest stage is fundamental to successful intervention.

Pastoral care is about genuine and honest relationships and therefore, understanding and practical help in themselves will not be sufficient, rather, an authentically conveyed identity with the desolation of the other is required. This can only be shown convincingly by an empathy that flows from our inner-selves which is grounded not in expertise but in mutuality.

Only by listening and absorbing the other's word, with complete acceptance can we provide for a psychodynamic environment in which God's love can reach the other. Useful to this work are images of the shepherd and the 'wounded healer' graphically displayed in the vulnerability and weakness of Christ, through which the power of love can be mediated. Coming to terms with our sufferings and needs, as carers, can be transformed by so doing into healing qualities in which pain is both accepted and shared.

It is clear from statistical evidence that both the young, especially adolescent girls and young men, and the old (primarily because of greater bereavement, isolation and ill health) are the groups which are high in risk factors and therefore in greatest need. As Christians, we believe in God's special concern for the weak and oppressed, and in the context of those driven to self-destruction, we must include the abused, lonely and the marginalised in society, the poor, troubled and those with reduced future prospects. God has concern for the well-being and salvation of all creatures and these have a special place, for His bias to the oppressed is not to the detriment of those who flourish but an expression of God's saving action at the heart of living.

Jesus taking up the role of the suffering servant provides in history not only essential solidarity with the wretched but also God's protest at innocent suffering. Theologically, the imperative is to ally ourselves with those at risk, the down-trodden and vulnerable, and through an empathic sharing with the 'heavy laden', show God's concern to all in society.

At the heart of our response should be a courageous spiritual commitment willing to live with all the risks of uncertainty of outcome associated with those who live 'on the edge'. Suicide for centuries has been misunderstood, seen primarily as a weak, self-centred, manipulative and selfish act. Today we are seeing signs of a greater understanding of suicide as a fundamental breakdown of living.

The suffering servant model that Christ portrays provides a compelling vision of God's saving initiative on earth, but the challenge to His people is demanding; not merely our collaboration is needed, we are we bidden to take responsibility for our despairing neighbour, whose continued life and welfare remains firmly in our hands. Awareness of this is of paramount importance.

2. Meeting the Crisis

In the face of such a challenge it would be easy to respond merely by exploring all the practical details involved in establishing direct targeted aid to those who, providing they can be readily identified, are at the gravest risk of self destruction. But, this is not a simple problem, for though it is possible to identify those categories of individuals who may be at risk, it is extremely difficult to predict who is likely to commit suicide.

Similarly, to meet the need, it would be too easy to propose that the Church initiates a professional cadre of Clergy or lay counsellors, all of whom would be skilled in various techniques, whose training and development would be financed by the Christian community. Again, we do not live in a world of infinite resources and I am not persuaded that such a proposal would necessarily identify the majority of sufferers nor, just as important, change the hearts and actions of Christians as a whole.

Also, from a purely functional view, the Church community is such that it operates best pastorally not at the macro level but at the parochial level. Therefore at this point, the priority lays in initiating not a welfare revolution from without so much as a spiritual transformation from within. Understanding and insight are required first before practical measures are envisaged, and to achieve this a broad educative approach is needed rooted in a 'theology of living'.

This might take the form of diocesan or ecumenically led commitments to help Christians in their respective church settings to understand more sensitively, using scriptural, sociological and psychological insights, the world of the suicidal. Such an educative process would acknowledge that (i) suicide represents, in its most tragic form, the result of a breakdown in living that afflicts many people of varying ages and backgrounds, and (ii) that Christians must be conscious of the theological imperative of shared suffering if they are to minister effectively to the anxious and despairing.

3. A Theology of Living

Such a theology of living would have three basic objectives (i) the inculcation of knowledge (ii) the influencing of attitudes (iii) the development of skills and strategies. These processes would aim to address the existing situation in which, so often, religious beliefs operate as a restrictive even censorial orthodoxy, instead of liberating challenge to our habitual ways and attitudes in the ministry of spiritual care and physical support to the needy.

(a) The Inculcation of Knowledge

Knowledge would include a broad insight into the collective and individual forces that affect the vulnerable in society: physical/cultural isolation, economic/political uncertainty, health and educational pressures, family and marital disintegration, unemployment, drug and alcohol abuse amongst the young.

More research would be needed to identify those who are 'poor copers' in the community, a significant amount of this can be drawn from local profiles once the issues have been raised in parishes. It would be essential, through the collection of statistical data to establish the full extent of need specifically amongst adolescents prone to D.S.H.

Common factors associated with suicide need to be widely recognised and understood: poor accommodation, undernourished backgrounds, apathy, loss of ties, lack of a realistic future and support from others, above all, the need for regular opportunities to talk in a friendly and supportive environment.

The absence of a concept of healthy living amongst the young will need to be remedied and since communication is a central problem in the development of suicidal crisis, this needs to be recognised and strategies developed to encourage the sharing of negative feelings.

External sustaining resources that have served to support the vulnerable can be threatened by the unexpected traumas of living: divorce, bereavement, loss of job or status, police or court cases, financial ruin. Carers need to be aware of these.

Despair also needs to be distinguished from depression, a condition that may be treatable by medical means and not necessarily associated with feelings of self destruction. Similarly, psychiatric illness which may be diagnosed clinically needs to be contrasted with the onset of psychiatric symptoms that sometimes accompany suicidal crisis.

Some knowledge of assessment risk is useful, though Prediction Intent Scales are only of value where careful evaluation is employed. There is a need for a 'resource unit' within established church structures to help provide information, expertise and encouragement to all who are caring for the despairing. If they are to be enabled to be effective pastoral carers then development of 'self knowledge' in all its forms is central.

The Christian Church sometimes tends towards a hiding of true feelings and motives, often under a veil of social respectability. Desiring to help is not sufficient in itself, more is demanded of us for we must learn to know our own fears and wounds through reflection. Here, the fostering of self-help groups, where those seeking to work with the suicidal can share worries and concerns, would be especially relevant.

To offer pastoral ministry to those experiencing such suffering is no easy task, for suicide alienates Christians because it represents failure and the ultimate negation of living. This is something that all of us are frightened to confront for fear that we may slip into the gloomy abyss of despair ourselves. We need therefore to adopt a theology of living that is itself sustained by spiritual development, which implies the inculcation of knowledge and continued prayer and reflection as a long term process.

Because our theology of living will daily be severely challenged by many self-deaths and numerous cases of D.S.H., it will be important to reflect this encounter adequately in our Christian way of life. Today we do not communicate with each other about suicide, we neither try to explain it to our congregations nor convey our attitudes to it to the world. Yet, in the shepherding model of the Healer who has known the dark world of despair, there is an important source of divine revelation that will benefit the hermeneutic of suffering.

I believe a pastorally active Church aware and struggling with the despair of others can be a Church deepened in a compelling way, in its understanding of God. Applying theology to the horrific phenomenon of despair called suicide, may yet yield an even richer insight into a living God who cares passionately about the individual in the context of society.

(b) The Influencing of Attitudes

Christian belief is not purely a private and individualistic matter. To neglect to influence attitudes in society at large, that are detrimental to a more compassionate view of the despairing, is to suffocate the work of the spirit.   Today, there are important questions for the Christian community to address if they are seeking seriously to change attitudes that may pave the way to a more caring nation.

For example, since one of the results of powerful measures to reduce inflation is a greater rise in redundancy and unemployment, then should there not be greater support for those who are put at risk?   If there is to be a drive toward reducing suicide by significantly large percentages then should the prescription of psychtropic drugs be actively reduced? Also, if government policies cause vast increases of the psychiatrically ill to be managed in the community then surely a prority must be to provide commensurate funding and aid.

The more we seek for those who are 'lost' and helpless, the more we need to go not further from the world, but more deeply into it. Poverty, isolation and depressive illness are symptomatic of the health of the nation in the very widest sense.   The world of human power, violence and injustice is where God suffers and we must not be deluded, for the fundamental result of greed, irresponsibility and lack of equity is chronic hopelessness.

Though this enquiry is not about ministry to the bereaved specifically, mention ought to be made of the importance of this work in the influencing of future generations to unexpected death. Both clergy and lay-folk are expected to help survivors through the various phases that form part of the grief process.

However, there are specific factors involved with the unresolved grief associated with suicide death.   Because it is so sudden and usually unexpected there is no preparation for the shock which is experienced as a devastating emotional blow. Sudden death, such as this, accelerates rates of change in domestic environment which in themselves can be physically and psychologically overwhelming.

Death by suicide is often violent and rejection of others is often implicit. Surviving relatives and friends often feel flooded with disturbing thoughts of vengeance and retribution. It is not unusual for survivors to be still angry many months or even years later.

Suicide engenders guilt in those remaining and since it frequently takes place in family systems already experiencing stress, then the act can produce disorders in the survivors. Death, in this way, can compromise the usual mourning rituals and may lead to harmful expressions of unconscious anger, survivors typically denying the rejection which can cause turmoil that itself blocks free communication.

Following suicide, the usual supports may be withdrawn and Christians can, if they are aware, take the place of some of these but it is an especially sensitive area. It will be the job of clergy primarily to help bolster faith at this critical juncture by influencing the attitudes of all concerned. Questions need to be answered honestly and simply: is suicide a sin? will the victim be judged harshly? where are they now? Such questions require knowledge of Biblical and theological belief but time is needed to explore these. A brief survey of existing thinking may be a useful beginning to understanding an experience that will undoubtedly change for ever the survivor's thinking.

Carers will need to have come to grips with their own feelings about suicide and since it is something that is rarely discussed, literature that helps exploration needs to be accessible. The carer, whilst attempting to establish a compassionate approach so as to set the stage for an open expression of grief to facilitate the bereavement process, is in a powerful position of influence. Their attitude and remarks can model a frank and undistorted response to the reality of suicide.

Whilst involving the family with the planning of liturgy is essential, it is also a valuable opportunity to sensitise the entire congregation to the phenomenon of suicide. The feelings commonly experienced by survivors: guilt, shame, anxiety, social isolation, anger and rage can be discussed so enabling laity to reach out and offer sensitive understanding and support.

Finally, it is important to realise that suicide ministry is a long-term commitment, if the initial involvement with survivors is effective then this provides a firm foundation for further help in the future. Speaking from my own experience, suicide can uncover a plethora of troubles with family relations but it can also be a turning point for the family. Lives are never to be the same, pain will have to be shared individually and corporately but this can provide great opportunities for deepening and re-examining faith as well as re-assessing the value of love and life.

(c) The Development of Skills and Strategies

The third and final objective in this educative process is the nurturing of skill-based strategies, the development and application of which can aid directly those called to minister. In this, I believe our priority must be the young, it is so often at this point in an individual's development that the first signs of unease and distraction begin to appear. Bearing in mind that a majority of those who engage in self-destructive behaviour will go on to more lethal attempts if left unchecked, it is important to treat every case as serious.

In Chapter three I set out my reasons for believing that schools can be the logical forum for the establishing of healthy patterns of discussion, sharing and referral where problems are arising. Central to this, is the question of communication. The emerging young commonly experience problems in confiding with adults just at that moment when they are engaged in the separating process that heralds a more independent outlook on life.

It is important for our response to first acknowledge that this is a widespread problem and that the crisis can be sensitively observed where typical symptoms are recognised and understood. Anxiety arising out of relationship problems, isolation and increased tension caused by bullying, change, long-term trauma, abuse, are all well documented factors that nevertheless can be masked by the onset of puberty.

Schools themselves need to be encouraged to develop an ethos that favours the sharing of confidences and a rapport that makes it easier for staff, chaplains, matrons, etc. to reach out. Clearly, not only data on the incidence of cases nationally is required in both schools and colleges, so also the establishment of report and referral policies, wider dissemination of useful advice and training in counselling skills.

Educational establishments will need, in addition, to foster a more positive self-concept amongst students that should include attention to self-esteem and control. Where there are tensions they will need to be addressed quickly, delay can contribute to a heightening of anxiety so provoking crisis. Adults themselves need to convey models in keeping with values associated with self acceptance and respect for others so that good and bad feelings may be expressed without threat.

What we are exploring here really is the establishing of a 'whole life' model of education that encourages both discussion and reflection on the experiences of growth, part of which can be powerful feelings of failure, dismay and self-destruction. Above all the intention must be to provide an environment where youth can express negative feelings rather than 'acting them out'.

Schools have long recognised the need for health education in the purely physical realm why separate out the emotional and spiritual from this? As adolescents continue to struggle with an increasingly complex and unsupportive environment such an educational focus grows more urgent. Since many young people confide in their peers it may be necessary to advise the young how to deal with confidences of a serious nature, not overreacting but encouraging talk without interruption, whilst negotiating help from trustworthy sources.

Such a school-centred, community-involved suicide education programme should be more than a preventative system but also a programme capable of enhancing and enriching life as well. Of course, this cannot and will not happen until anxiety and fear about death is reduced to a manageable level. Suicide has been a fact of life for millennia, developing an open attitude to it is not to encourage it, but rather, in thinking honestly about it, we may actually decrease people's capacity for suicidal behaviour.

The second of the seven principles of the Samaritans reads: 'The Samaritans also seek to alleviate human misery, loneliness, despair and depression by listening and befriending those who feel they have no one else to turn to who would understand and accept them.' A better definition of Christian love is difficult to imagine, save for 'love your neighbour as yourself.'

To do all of these things does require, however, that self-love which is totally accepting, born of the real experience of living sometimes in black despair. Who amongst us can say with any certainty that we will not be called upon to assist with such a ministry in the future?

CONCLUSION

The essential concern of this enquiry has been with the apparent lack of an informed and accessible pastoral resource, available both to clergy and laity, that might aid them in ministering to those contemplating suicide. Familiar with the trauma of suicide, I was aware that though valuable and solid materials exist to assist bereavement counselling, there was a noticeable absence of research that linked the wider theological, sociological and psychological aspects of voluntary death.

My intention therefore, in surveying critically these various disciplines, all of which have important things to say about self-destruction, was to provide not only a broad body of knowledge, but a relevant perspective from which a resource might emerge appropriate to the needs of the Christian carer. In undertaking this study it has become clear that self-inflicted death is not new, but nevertheless, remains a largely hidden phenomenon of the life experience of human society. Indeed, its 'hiddenness' has not only in part contributed towards its neglect as a cause for serious concern, but in church circles it ceased long ago to be a theme thought suitable for more explicit theological reflection.

It remains my belief, that at a time when national statistics for suicide and deliberate self-harm continue to rise alarmingly, the Church needs to re-examine its own role in ministering to the anxious and despairing. By so doing, Christian responses will have not only helped uncover the shared pain and suffering of human living, but reveal the essential nature of Christ's sacrifice for humankind, that provides the model and the pattern for pastoral ministry.

Appendixes

CONFIDENTIAL

NOVEMBER 1993

APPENDIX 1
SPECIMEN PROFILE FORM

QUESTIONNAIRE

AIM: To establish numbers and circumstances, where known, of suicides and/or attempted suicides in Parishes of the Witney Deanery
During a 5 year period
(Calendar years January 1988 – December 1993)

Name of Clergy...

Name of Parish...

	Sex (M/F)	Marital Status	Suicide or Attempted (with approx. date)	Any previous attempts (give number if possible)	Specific Methods (see* below)	Religious Affiliation as Church goer/how long
1.						
2.						
3.						
4.						
5.						
6.						
7.						
8.						

*poisoning by solid/liquid substances; gases/vapours; hanging/strangling/suffocation; drowning; firearms/explosives; falls from high places; burns/scalds; other

APPENDIX 1 (b)

Suicide/Attempted Suicide

Case Profile No: **Parish:**

From your knowledge of the individual concerned, please indicate whether the following factors were present during/before the attempt and add any relevant detail:

No.1.   Any previous illness, mental/physical?

No. 2.   Did the individual appear in any way vulnerable?

No.3.   How would you describe their personality, normally and/or before the attempt?

No.4.   Was there evidence of depression?

No.5.   Had the individual suffered any recent trauma?

No.6.   Would you describe them as isolated, lacking meaningful contact with others?

No.7.   How would you describe their literacy/education?

No.8.   Describe their behaviour before and running up to the attempt.

No.9.   Were there problems in their physical conditions of living, housing/dependents?

No.10.   Were there major problems of a financial nature?

No.11.   Occupation, retired or unemployed?

No.12.   Any evidence of alcohol/drug abuse?

No.13.   Any evidence of hypochondria/attention seeking/

No.14.   Any evidence of marital breakdown?

No.15.   Any evidence of having been in prison, awaiting court case, bail?

No.16.   Broken relationships/family problems/broken home in childhood?

No.17.   General appearance (fastidious, smart, scruffy, unkempt)?

No.18.   Was there a tendency to talk about suicide?

No.19.   Ethnic origin.

No.20.   Other significant information.

APPENDIX 1 (a)

For each case we shall be considering the following factors that may have contributed to the act:

Illness: mental (including alcohol/drug misuse)
physical (including painful, life-threatening or disabling illness)

Personal factors: lack of social support; attitude to suicide; broken relationships etc.

Stressful life events: loss of job; divorce; bereavement; imprisonment; migration; diagnosis of illness; traumatic shock; involvement in war.

Changes in wider cultural environment: economic climate, cultural attitudes.

Access to means of committing suicide.

APPENDIX 2 (a)

LOCAL SURVEY

Survey to establish numbers and circumstances (where known) of suicides/attempted suicides presented to the Clergy of the Witney Deanery during a five year period (Calendar years since January 1988- December 1993)

Numbers:

Areas	Staff St.N/s	Electoral Roll	Population	No. Suicides	Att/Suicides	Total
1.Witney	4 1	342	20,000	1	-	1
2.Ducklington	1 1	242	1535	1	1	2
3.MinsterLovell	1	88	2100	1	-	1
4.Cogges	2	225	4740	2	-	2
5.Carterton	2	172	14,000	6	1	7
6.Burford	1 1	254	1999	2	2	4
7.Swinbrook	1	41	450	-	-	-
8.Alvescot	1	97	910	1	-	1
9.Bampton	1	176	4115	1	-	1
10.Broadshires	1	165	1040	3	-	3
11.Standlake	1	131	2419	-	-	-
11 Areas	19	1933	53,308	18	4	22
Additional :	2 new	Staff members		3 cases	From previous parishes	
Retired Clergy:					No cases	

APPENDIX 2 (b)

DETAILS OF INDIVIDUAL CASES

Area	Approx Age	Sex	Marital Status	Attempted Suicide	Suicide	Previous Attempts	Method	Church Affiliation	Year
1.(a)	51	M	m		+	-	Gas	Church Warden5yrs	1988
2.(a)	14	F	s	+		-	Cut Wrists	Yes	1993
2.(b)	36	M	m		+	-	Hanging	Nil	1990's
3.(a)	32	M	m		+	1	Gas	Fringe	1993
4.(a)	25	M	m		+	-	Exhaust	Nil	1992
4.(b)	40	M	m		+	?	Unclear	Nil	1993
5.(a)	30	M	m		+	?	Firearm	Nil	1988
5.(b)	30	F	m		+	?	Firearm	Nil	1988
5.(c)	23	M	s		+	?	Firearm	Nil	1988
5.(d)	75	M	s		+	?	Drowning	Yes	1988
5.(e)	22	M	s		+	?	Poisoning	Nil	1989
5.(f)	32	F	d		+	?	Poisoning	Nil	1991
5.(g)	25	F	s	+		3	Cut/burns Scalds	Yes	1993/4
6.(a)	78	M	w		+	?	Suffocated	Yes	1993
6.(b)	75	M	m	+		?	Solids	Nil	1993
6.(c)	50	M	m		+	2	Poisoning Exhaust	Nil	1992
6.(d)	13	M	s	+		-	Poisoning	Yes	1993
7.	-	-	-	+		-	-	-	-
8.(a)	43	M	s		+	-	Poisoning	Nil	1993
9.(a)	18	F	s		+	-	Poisoning	Nil	1989
10a)	70	M	s		+	-	Firearm	Nil	1988
10b)	56	F	m		+	1	Firearm	Yes	1989
10c)	58	M	M		+	-	Firearm	Nil	1993

F	Female
M	Male
d	divorced
w	widowed
m	married
s	single

APPENDIX 2 (c)

Documented and other factors which were present
during/before the attempt and which may have
contributed to the act of suicide/attempted suicide

Area and Case	Suicide A/Suicide	Previous Illness	Considered Vulnerable	Perceived Personality	Evidence of Depression
1.(a)	S	No	No	Confident	No
2.(a)	A/S	No	Yes	Introvert	Yes
2.(b)	S	No	No	Outgoing/ pressurised	No
3.(a)	S	No	Yes	Neurotic	Yes
4.(a)	S	No	-	-	-
4.(b)	S	Disabled –Work accident	Yes	-	-
5.(a)	Joint S?	No	Yes-child in	Intense	Coping
5.(b)	Ditto	No	house fire	Intense	Coping
5.(c)	S	No	Loner-good family	-	No but worried
5.(d)	S	Emphysema elderly/frail	Yes	Enjoyed life	Yes
5.(e)	S	Schizophrenia	Spell as in-patient/heard voices	Normal	Moody
5.(f)	S	Diabetic	Yes/temper	Outgoing	Moody
5.(g)	A/S	Clinical depression/asthma	Yes/doubts re.sexual orientation	Shy/lacking confidence/ selfworth	Yes chronic
6.(a)	S	Yes	No	Reserved	No
6.(b)	A/S	No	No	Reserved	No
6.(c)	S	Yes psychiatric symptoms	Yes	Angry Selfcentred	Yes
6.(d)	A/S	Evidence of counselling	Yes insecure	Extrovert not settled	No
8.(a)	S	No	Yes	Tense/ difficult	No
9.(a)	S	No	-	-	-
10a)	S	Depression	Yes	-	Yes
10b)	S	Depression	Yes	Open/ friendly	Yes
10c)	S	Terminal cancer/ Given 18 months	-	Strongwilled obstinate	-

Area And Case	Any Recent Trauma	Appear Isolated	Education	Behaviour Preceding	Living Conditions
1.(a)	Yes, bailiffs removed furniture	No	Good	Normal	At risk
2.(a)	Breakup with boyfriend	No	Good	Withdrawn	O.K.
2.(b)	Yes Business collapse	No	Very Good	Under stress	O.K.
3.(a)	-	Yes/partially	Basic	Erratic	Accom/ion Changes
4.(a)	-	-	-	-	-
4.(b)	-	Lived with wife	-	-	-
5.(a)	Child death	Yes/Gamekeeper	Good	Normal	Accom/ion
5.(b)	Lost home	No/pub work	Good	Normal	Rented
5.(c)	Under Police Invest/ion	Yes	Good	Normal	O.K.
5.(d)	Long illness/not go on	Lived alone but contact with others	Bright	Normal	O.K.
5.(e)	No	Yes	Not bright	Going through a bad patch	O.K. mother depressed
5.(f)	Argument with parent divorce/ court proceeding	Yes	Bright	Anger	Single parent child with grand-parents
5.(g)	Family abuse brother in prison	Feels very isolated	Poor	Distressed	Poor
6.(a)	Death of wife	No	Excellent	Normal	O.K.
6.(b)	No	No	Excellent	Quietly depressed	O.K.
6.(c)	Court case divorce	Yes living apart	Good	Manic/ depressed	Could not cope
6.(d)	Molested School change	Not good at socialising with peers	Average	Anxious unsettled	Boarding School Stressful
	Continued	Over			

8.(a)	Not recent	No long-term relationships	Good	-	Lived alone
9.(a)	-	Happy	Good	Normal	O.K.
10a)	-	Withdrawn	Limited	-	Large/cold farmhouse
10b)	No	No	Good	Unsettled	O.K.
10c)	Terminal diagnosis	Strongly individualistic	Excellent	Bloody-minded	Scruffy cottage

Area And Case	Financial Problems	Occupation	Alcohol Misuse	Attention Seeking	Marital Breakdown
1.(a)	Yes serious	Company Director	No	Yes	No
2.(a)	No	At school	No	-	Temporary Break-up of parents
2.(b)	Yes serious	Self-employed	Yes	No	No
3.(a)	-	unemployed	Yes	-	Yes separated
4.(a)	-	Labourer	-	-	-
4.(b)	-	Unemployed disability	-	-	-
5.(a)	No	Unemployed	-	-	Possibly rumour wife's affair
5.(b)	-	barmaid	-	-	-
5.(c)	No	Office worker	No	No	single
5.(d)	No	Retired	Yes	No	-
5.(e)	No	Worked with father	No	No	-
5.(f)	Yes enormous	Advisor Diabetic unit	No	No	Yes
5.(g)	poor	Unemployed	No	Yes	-
6.(a)	No	Retired	No	No	No
6.(b)	No	Retired	No	No	No
6.(c)	Yes	Retired early Health grounds Then unemployed.	Yes/drugs	Yes	Yes
6.(d)	No	-	-	Talking about drugs & sexuality	No
8.(a)	No	Electrical mechanic	Drugs	No	No
9.(a)	-	Student	No	No	Broke-up With boyfriend.
10a)	Yes	Farmer	-	-	-
10b)	No	Farmer's wife	-	-	-
10c)	No	Unemployed	Yes	No	Unhappy

Area and case	Court case	Strained Family Relationships	Appearance	Ethnic origin
1.(a)	No	No	Smart	British
2.(a)	No	Yes	Normal Teenager	British
2.(b)	No	No	Smart	British
3.(a)	No	Yes	Average	British
4.(a)	-	-	-	British
4.(b)	-	-	-	British
5.(a)	-	Refused help	Smart	British
5.(b)	-	Child caused fire	Very Smart	British
5.(c)	Yes but trivial	No	Smart	British
5.(d)	-	No	Smart	British
5.(e)	-	No	O.K.	British
5.(f)	Court case day before	No	Smart	British
5.(g)	Court case Brother/father	Strained family relationships	Scruffy but clean	British
6.(a)	No	No	Smart	Jewish
6.(b)	No	No	Smart	British
6.(c)	Divorce/police case	Poor upbringing Marital disharmony	Scruffy unclean	British
6.(d)	No	Insecure when young/when moving home	Normally Smart – unkempt	British
8.(a)	No	No	-	British
9.(a)	No	No	-	English descent
10a)	-	-	-	-
10b)	-	-	Smart	British
10c)	No	No	Untidy	British

Area and case	Tendency to talk about suicide	Other
1.(a)	No	Secretive about problems
2.(a)	Yes to peer group	-
2.(b)	No	-
3.(a)	Yes	Wife unwilling to start family, hence break-up
4.(a)	-	Insufficient background known
4.(b)	-	Secretive, neighbours not notified of funeral, wife refused all help from clergy or doctor
5.(a)	No	Probably killed wife first then suicide
5.(b)	No	She had worked that evening
5.(c)	No	-
5.(d)	No	-
5.(e)	No	Though he did not talk about suicide, he was Reading about life after death at the time
5.(f)	No	Though she did not talk about suicide, preparations were very determined and precise – bonfire of documents, flat spotlessly clean
5.(g)	Yes	Generally unhappy, lacking self-worth mentally and physically unwell
6.(a)	No	Suffering terminal cancer DIY suicide suspected
6.(b)	No	-
6.(c)	Yes	Displaying all the symptoms associated with anxiety and worthlessness
6.(d)	No	This appears to have been an impulsive attempt to draw attention to an earlier problem, appeared not to be able to share with parents
8.(a)	No	His brother (SAS) killed 12 years previously, had a shattering effect upon him, left the navy after alcohol problem
9.(a)	-	-
10a)	-	-
10b)	Yes	-
10c)	Yes	Suicide seen as the final solution, method considered by many as done for effect

APPENDIX 3

SUICIDAL INTENT SCALE

Beck, A.T., Schuyler, D and Herman, J.

1974   'Development of Suicidal Intent Scales'. In The Prediction of Suicide. Eds. A.T., Beck, H.L.P. Resnick and D. J. Lettieri. Maryland: Charles Press.

Developed to help measure degree of suicidal intent associated with an attempt. First section deals with the circumstances surrounding the attempt and the second section the individual's expectations and feelings at the time. It includes 15 items, each one scores 0, 1, or 2 points. Total Score (0-30) is used to assess the intent i.e. high score = high suicide intent. The scale is easy to administer and can be incorporated into an interview.

Part 1 Objective circumstances related to suicide attempt

1. Isolation   0 = somebody present; 1 = somebody nearby or in visual/vocal contact; 2 = no one nearby or in visual/vocal contact.

2. Timing   0 = intervention probably; 1 = intervention unlikely; 2 = intervention highly unlikely

3. Precautions against discovery/intervention 0 = no precaution; 1 = passive precautions (e.g. avoiding others but doing nothing to prevent their intervention; alone in room with unlocked door; 2 = active precautions (e.g. locked door)

4. Acting to get help during/after attempt 0 = notified potential helper regarding attempt; 1 = contacted but did not specifically notify potential helper regarding attempt; 2 = did not contact or notify potential helper.

5. Final acts in anticipation of death (e.g. will, gifts, insurance) 0 = none; 1 = thought about it or made some arrangements; 2 = definite plans/completed arrangements

6. Active preparation for attempt 0 = none; 1 = minimal to moderate; 2 = extensive.

7. Suicide Note 0 = absence of note; 1 = note written but torn up, or thought about. 2 = presence of note.

8. Overt Communication of intent before the attempt 0 = none; 1 = equivocal communication; 2 = unequivocal communication

Part 2 Self Report

9. Alleged purpose of attempt. 0 = to manipulate environment; get attention, revenge 1 = components of '0' and '2'; 2 = to escape, to solve problems.

10. Expectation of fatality 0 = thought that death was unlikely; 1 = thought that death was possible but not probable; 2 = thought that death was probable/certain

11. Conception of method's lethality 0 = did less to self than thought would be lethal; 1 = was unsure if action would be lethal; 2 = equalled or exceeded what he thought would be lethal.

12 Seriousness of attempt 0 = did not seriously attempt to end life; 1 = uncertain about seriousness to end life; 2 = seriously attempted to end life.

13. Attitude toward living/dying 0 = did not want to die; 1 = components of '0' and '2'; 2 = wanted to die.

14. Conception of medical rescuability 0 = thought that death with be unlikely with medical attention; 1 = was uncertain whether death could be overted by medical attention; 2 = was certain of death even with medical attention.

15. Degree of pre-meditation 0 = none, impulsive; 1 = contemplated for 3 hours or less before attempt; 2 = contemplated for more than 3 hours before attempt.

When motivational aspects of attempted suicide are considered the extent of suicidal intent as measured by Beck's Suicidal Intent Scale was found to be more closely associated with the presence of feelings of Hopelessness rather than with the degree of depression (Wetzel, 1976:1069)

Beck et.al. also discovered that among depressed patients admitted to hospital with suicidal ideas, levels of hopelessness at the time of admission were a better predictor of risk of eventual suicide than was the severity of depression. A scale is available to evaluate hopelessness. (Beck et.al. 1974:861)

APPENDIX 4 (a)

RELEVANT ORGANISATIONS

British Association for Counselling
1 Regent Place
Rugby
CV21 2PJ
Tel. 01788 578328 (Information line)
**   550899 (Office)**

Although it does not provide counselling services directly, BAC is able to provide callers with information on how to obtain access to a counsellor in their local area. Publications include an Information Sheet entitled 'What is Counselling?' and 'A client's Guide to Counselling and Psychotherapy'. Telephone enquiries can be made, although BAC prefers to receive enquiries in writing (with stamped addressed envelope please).

The Compassionate Friends
53 North Street
Bristol
BS3 1EN
Tel. 0117 9539639 (Helpline)   0117 9665202 (Administration)

The Compassionate Friends is a nationwide self-help organisation of *parents whose child of any age (including adult) has died from any cause.* TCF offers personal and group support and befriending (but not counselling). There is a quarterly newsletter, a postal library and a range of leaflets. TCF contact list includes SOS (Shadow of Suicide) contacts in some parts of the country.

CRUSE
Cruse House
126 Sheen Road
Richmond, Surrey
TW9 1UR
Tel. 0181 840 4818   0181 332 7227 (Cruse Bereavement Line)

CRUSE Bereavement Care is a national organisation which offers help to all bereaved people through its local branches and national office. It has nearly 200 branches *offering individual counselling as well as social support and advice on practical matters relating to bereavement.* Wherever possible, enquirers will be directed to their local CRUSE branch. Where no local branch exists, head office offers a link with a counsellor by letter or by telephone via the Bereavement Line. CRUSE has a wide range of publications on various aspects of bereavement. There is *Cruse Chronicle,* a newsletter for members, and *bereavement Care*, a journal for professionals who work with the dying and the bereaved.

INQUEST
Ground Floor
Alexandra National House
330 Seven Sisters Road
London N4 2PJ
Tel. 0181 802 7430

INQUEST is concerned with *deaths in custody, psychiatric or special hospitals, deaths at work and those* involving issues of public health and safety. Free legal and advice service to bereaved people.

Jewish Bereavement Counselling Service
Visitation Committee
Woburn House
Tavistock Square
London WC1H)EZ
Tel. 0171 387 4300 ext. 277 (Office Hours)
**   0181 349 0829 (24-hour ansaphone)**

This service offers *counselling and support to members of the Jewish community who are bereaved.* People are visited in their own homes by trained volunteer counsellors. At present, the Jewish Bereavement Counselling Service operates mainly in North West and South West London and in Redbridge (Essex).

Lesbian and Gay Bereavement Project
Vaughan M. Williams Centre
Colindale Hospital
London
NW9 5HG
Tel. 0181 200 0511 (Office)
          0181 455 8894 (Helpline, see below)

The project offers telephone counselling for lesbians and gay men *bereaved by the loss of a same-sex partner*, or otherwise affected by bereavement. A member is on duty every evening from 7 pm to midnight, and can be contacted via the helpline number listed above. The project also publishes a will form and can often find suitable clergy or secular officiants for funerals. Speakers and discussion leaders can be provided for any group concerned with issues relating to death and dying.

London Association of Bereavement Services
London Voluntary Sector Resources Centre
356 Holloway Road
London N7 6PN
Tel. 0171 700 8134

LABS is an umbrella organisation for over 100 bereavement services and associate members in the *Greater London Area*. They can assist enquirers with locating their nearest and most appropriate bereavement service.

NAFSIYAT
278 Seven Sisters Road
London N4 2HY
Tel. 0171 263 4130

NAFSIYAT is an inter-cultural therapy centre offering a range of different psychotherapies. The majority of its current users life in the

London Borough of Islington, but referrals (including self-referrals) can be accepted from elsewhere.   NAFSIYAT has worked with individuals, couples and families from many different ethnic groups.   The centre is able to offer some consultation and assessment services to professionals in other services.   The centre also offers counselling and psychotherapy training.

National Association of Bereavement Services
20 North Folgate
London E1 6DB
Tel. 0171 247 1080 (Referrals)   0171 247 0617 (Administration)

NABS is a support organisation for bereavement services and acts as a *referral agency by putting bereaved people in touch with their nearest most appropriate local services.*   It was founded in 1988 to bring together *individuals and groups who are actively involved in the care of the dying and bereaved.* NABS promotes networking, training and professional standards. It produces a quarterly newsletter and holds an annual training conference.

The Samaritans
10 The Grove
Slough
Berkshire
SL1 1QP
Tel. 01753 53212 (Administration)
**   0345 90 90 90 (single number for callers; charged at local rate)**

The Samaritans operate in the UK and the Republic of Ireland. They are available at any hour of the day or night to *befriend those passing through personal crisis or in imminent danger of taking their own lives.*   Their telephone service, which is confidential, operates every day of the year. There are around 200 branches throughout the UK and Ireland which are staffed by 23,000 volunteers. Anyone wishing to contact them may do so by telephoning or by calling in at their local branch. In addition to the telephone service, all local branches are able to offer face-to-face befriending during the daytime.

120   Christopher Tadman-Robins

AN A-Z OF HELP: Sources of Support for
Young People with Specific Problems or Needs

Acceptance – A helpline and support group for parents of lesbians and gay men. Tel. 0795 661463 Tuesday – Friday 7 p.m. to 9 p.m.

ADFAM National – Support and information about drugs and related services in the UK for drug users and their families. 1ˢᵗ Floor, Upworth Huse, 25 City Road, London EC1Y. Tel. 0171 638 3700 (Helpline 10-5 weekdays)

Al-anon Family Groups UK and Eire 61 Great Dover Street, London SE1 4YF. Tel. 0171 403 0888 (24 hour helpline).   Support for those (relatives/friends) affected by a problem drinker. 1,090 groups in UK. Alateen based at the same address offers help to teenagers affected by alcoholics, usually parents.

Alateen – Help for young people aged 12-20 who have relatives or friends with alcohol problems. Information about local groups is available from 61 Great Dover Street, London SE1 4YF. Tel. 0171 403 0999 (24 hours a day)

Alcohol Concern, Waterbridge House, 32-36 Loman Street, London SE1 0EE. Tel. 0171 833 3471

Alcohol Counselling Service, 34 Electric Lane, London SW9 8JT. Tel. 0171 928 7377

Alcoholics Anonymous General Service office UK, PO Box 1, Stonebow House, York YO1 2NJ. Tel. 0904 644026 Help for those who want to stop drinking – a group therapy approach. (Local contacts/groups in phone book).

British Association of Psychotherapists. Psychoanalytical and psychotherapy service. 37 Mapesbury Toad, London NW2 4HJ. Tel. 0181 452 9823

Brook Advisory Centres Advice on pregnancy and contraception (see phone book for local numbers). 7 Belgrave Road, London SW1V 1QB. Tel. 0171 828 2484

Childline Telephone helpline for children and adolescents. Freepost 1111, London N1 0BR. (Free 24-hour phone service which will not show up on itemised telephone bills.)

Families Anonymous – Helpline for those who are worried about a family member's use of drugs. May be able to put you in contact with a self-help group in your area. The Doddington and Rollo Community Association, Charlote despard Avenue, London SW11 5JE. Tel. 0171 498 4680.

Family Planning Association Advice on pregnancy and contraception, 27 Mortimer Street, London W1N 7RJ. Tel. 071 636 7866. See phone book for local numbers.

Gay Bereavement Project Support and advice for people bereaved by death of same-sex partner. Vaughan M. Williams Centre, Colindale Hospital, London NW9 5HG Tel. 0181 200 0511 (Office) 0181 455 8894 (Helpline)

Gingerbread A national network of local mutual aid groups providing emotional support, practical help and social activities for one-parent families. 35 Wellington Street, London WC2E 7BN. Tel. 0171 240 0953

Jewish Bereavement Counselling Service Counselling and support to members of the Jewish community who are bereaved, mainly operated in North West and South West London . 1 Cyprus Gardens, London N3 1SP Tel. 0171 387 4300 ext. 277 (Office Hours) 0181 349 0829 (24-hour ansaphone)

Lesbian and Gay Switchboard   0171 837 7324

Lesbian Information Service (LIS) Information and help for lesbian women. Publish a 'coming-out' pack for young lesbians. PO Box 8, Todmorden, Lancs OL14 5TZ Tel. 0706 817235

MIND (National Association of Mental Health) Includes an information and advice service. Granta House, 15-19 Broadway, Stratford, London E15 4BQ Tel. 0181 519 2122

Mindlink MIND'S network for those that use mental health serVICES. Publishes a quarerly newsletter, *Mindwaves*.

NAFSIYAT The inter-cultural therapy centre offering a range of different psychotherapies working with individuals from many different ethnic groups (mostly in the Islington area). 278 Seven Sisters Road, London, N4 2HY
Tel. 0171 263 4130

Narcotics Anonymous Self-help organisation for those who have a problem with drugs, based on local meeting. Telephone advice given by recovering addicts. PO Box 1980, London N19 3LS. Tel. 0171 498 9005. (Advice line 10 a.m. to 10 pm every day)

National Aids Helpline 0800 567 123 (Free – 24 hour)

National Association of Bereavement Services refers individuals to bereavement support services in their area. 20 Norton Folgate, London E1 6DB Tel. 0171 247 0617

National Children's Home Action for Children Offers support to young people with a range of problems and can give contact numbers for help with specific problems. Tel. 0171 226 2033. Some local numbers are available from this national number.

NAYPCAS (The National Association of Young People's Counselling and Advisory Services) 17-23 Albion Street, Leicester LE1 6GD Tel. 0553 558 763. Can put you in touch with local youth counselling service. Include SAE.

NORCAP (National Organisation of Counselling for Adoptees) 3 New High Street, Headington, Oxford OX3 1AJ. Tel. 01865 750 554 (10 a.m. to 4 p.m. Mon, Wed, Fri.)

Northern Ireland Association for Mental Health (NIAMH) Beacon House, 80 University Street, Belfast BT7 1HE. Tel. 01232 328 474

NSF Formerly called the National Schizophrenia Fellowship, NSF provides information, support and an advice-line to support those whose lives are affected by schizophrenia. Self-help groups exist. NSFL 28 Castle Street, Kingston-upon-Thames, KT1 1SS. Advice line 081 974 6814   **NSF (Scotland):** 40 Shandick Place, Edinburgh EH2 4RT   Tel. 031 226 2025.

NSF (Northern Ireland) 37-39 Queen Street, Belfast BT1 6EA> Tel. 01232 248006

NSPCC Child Protection Helpline Support and advice for young people who have been abused or for anyone worried about a young person's safety. offers the chance to talk confidentially to trained social workers and receive advice on what to do next.   Tel. 0800 800 500 24 hour service, free calls that will not appear on an itemised telephone bill.

PACE (Project for Advice, Counselling and Education) London Lesbian and Gay Centre, 34 Hartham Road, London N7 Tel. 0171 700 1323

Parents' Friend. Helpline and support group for parents of lesbians and gay men. c/o 36 Newmarket, Otley, West Yorkshire. LS21 3AE. Tel. 01532 674627 (7.30 p.m. – 11 p.m.)

Positively Women Self-help group for women who are HIV positive or have AIDS. 5 Sebastian Street, London EC1V OHE. Tel. 1071 490 2327

Rape Crisis Rape Crisis centres are listed in local directory. They provide contact numbers for 'Action Against Incest' groups where these exist. Tel. 0171 837 1600 (London) or 0141 221 8448 (Glasgow)

Relate Specialises in helping people with relationship difficulties, whether married or single. London Office 76a New Cavendish Street, London W1. Tel. 0171 580 1087 Local addresses in phone book.

RELEASE Advice on legal problems arising from drug misuse. 388 Old Street, London EC1V 9LT. Tel. 1071 729 5255. Emergency telephone 0171 603 6854

RESOLV (The Society for the Prevention of Solvent and Volatile Substance Abuse) A charity solely concerned with solvent misuse. They publish leaflets, booklets and videos and know about local agencies who can help. 30A High Street, Stone Staffordshire. ST15 8AW. Tel. 01785 817 885

Saneline   Trained volunteers provide information and support to those suffering serious mental health problems and to their relatives and friends. Advice is available about local services and organisations. SANE, 2nd floor,

199-205 Old Marylebone Road, London NW1 5QP.   SANELINE: 0171
724 8000 (2 p.m. to midnight, every day.)

Scottish Association for Mental Health (SAMH)   Atlantic House, 38
Gardeners Crescent, Edinburgh EH3 8DG Tel. 01450 371 694/ 0131 229
9687

Terrence Higgins Trust Counselling, welfare and legal help for people
with AIDS and their friends and families. Tel. 0171 831 0330. Helpline
0171 242 1010 (12 noon – 10 p.m.)

Young Carers Project Supports research and development work for carers
who are school age and below and produces the *Young Carers Link*
Newsletter.   c/o Carers National Association, 20-25 Glasshouse Yard,
London EC1A 4JS.   Tel. 0171 490 8818: Carers Line 0171 490 8898

Young Minds Provides information about the national and local services
available to young people. This organisation is trying to establish a national
telephone helpline for adults who are worried about a young person's
feelings, thoughts or behaviour. 22A Boston Place, London NW1 6ER.
Tel. 0171 724 7262.

Youth Access Provides help and information to young people and their
parents about the youth counselling, advice and befriending services that are
available in their local area. Magazine Business Centre, 11 Newark Street,
Leicester. LE1 5SS. Tel. 01533 558763

APPENDIX 4 (b)

Suicide
And
Self
Harm

SASH

A resource within the Diocese concerned with issues of deliberate self harm and suicide

Lord, make us instruments of your peace
Where there is hatred, let us show love,
Where there is injury, pardon,
Where there is despair, hope
Where there is sadness, job

Grant heavenly Father,
That in every situation in life and in death
Your love may speak through us all to your people,
In their joy and their pain,
In their fear and their hope.
Amen.

The national helpline number for the Samaritans is

0345 90 90 90

For the cost of a local call.

How to contact SASH

The following clergy are involved in SASH and would welcome additions to the group:

Ivor Cornish (Chairman)
01296 630 345

Neil Lewis
01734 262 372

Julia Wilkinson
01494 531 141

Mervyn Eden
01753 525 962

Chris Tadman-Robins
01993 823 551

Georgie Simpson
01865 775 160

SASH is also linked to the Rural Stress Information Network
01203 412 916

The Facts

! Suicide ranks amongst the top ten cause of death in most European countries

! Suicide in young men has risen ten-fold in some areas between 1974 and is still rising.

! Some occupations suffer from disproportionately high suicide rates. These include vets, farmers, doctors, dentists and pharmacists

! Unemployment, a history of mental illness, misuse of drugs and alcohol, may all increase the risk of suicide.

! Parasuicide (Deliberate Self Harm) is one of the most common causes of overnights stays in hospitals in Oxfordshire.

The Challenge to the Church

! Published figures suggest that over a five-year period, most clergy teams will experience at least one suicide within their parish.

! A study in Oxfordshire found that 13% of those who deliberately self harmed had contacted clergy within the preceding week

! Clergy and others are often aware of cases of depression and potentially suicidal people.

How SASH can help

SASH (Suicide and Self Harm) is a group of clergy within the Diocese who have an interest in suicide and self harm. SASH exists to:

! Support clergy and others who are pastorally involved in situations involving suicide or DSH

! Raise aware ness of the problems of stress and suicide so that the church is better informed.

! Compile resources, especially liturgical, that will be of assistance to anyone involved in taking the funeral of a suicide victim.

! Organise training for those interested in mental health.

BIBLIOGRAPHY

Adelstein, A. & Mardon, C. 1975. 'Suicides *1961-74'* *Population Census & Census Trends 2* (1975 Winter).

Alderson, M. R. 1974. 'Self-poisoning: What's the Future?' *Lancet 1* (1974), 1040-3.

Aldridge, D. *1998. Suicide – The Tragedy of Hopelessness* London: Jessica Kingsley Publishers.

Alvarez, A. 1971. *The Savage God - A Study of Suicide.* London: Penguin.

Ambrose. 1896. *Selected Works and Letters.* Trans. H. Romestin. Oxford: James Parker.

Andersberg, Thomas. 1989 *Suicide-Definitions, Causes and Values.* Sweden: Lund U. Press.

Anderson, B. W. 1966. *The Living World of the Old Testament.* Sec.Edn. New Jersey: Longman.

Arieti, S. 1981. *Understanding and Helping The Schizophrenic -A Guide for Family and Friends.* Harmondsworth: Penguin

Aristotle, B.W. 1926 *Nichomachean Ethics.* Trans. H. Rackman Mass: Harvart U. Press.

Augustine. 1972 *City of God.* Trans. H. Bettenson London:

Bancroft, J., Reynolds, F., Simkin, S., Smith, J. 1975 'Self-poisoning and self-injury in the Oxford Area'. *British Journal of Preventative and Social Medicine 29* (1975), 170-7.

Bancroft, J. & Marsack, P. 1977. 'The Repetitiveness of Self-Poisoning and self-injury'. *British Journal of Psychiatry* 131 (1977), 394-9.

Bancroft, J., Skrimshire, S., Casson, A.., Harard-Watts, J., Reynolds, F. 1987. 'People who deliberately poison or injure themselves: their problems and their contacts with helping agencies'. *Psychological Medicine 7* (1977), 289-303.

Bancroft , J. 1979. 'Crisis Intervention'. *An Introduction to the Psychotherapies.* Ed. S. Bloch. Oxford: OUP: 83-101.

Bancroft, J., Skrimshire, A., Casson, J., Harvard-Watts., D. and Reynolds, F. 1977. 'People who deliberately poison or injure themselves: their problems and their contacts with helping agencies'. *Psychological Medicine 7, 289-303*

Barraclough, B., Bunch, J., Melson, B., Sainsbury, P. 1974. 'A Hundred cases of Suicide: Clinical Aspects'. *British Journal of Psychiatry* 125 (1974), 355-73.

Barry, F.R. 1966. *Christian Ethics and Secular Society.* London: Hodder & Stoughton Ltd.

Barth, Karl. 1961. *Church Dogmatics III.* Edinburgh: T. & T. Clark.

Beck, A.T., Resmick, H.L.P., Lettieri, J.D. 1974a. *The Prediction of Suicide.* Maryland: The Charles Press Publishers Inc.

Beck, A. T., Weissman, A., Lester, D., Trexler, L. 1974b. 'The Measurement of Pessimism: The Hopelessness Scale'. *Journal of Clinical Psychology 42* (1974), 861-5

Beck, A.T., Beck, R., Kovacs, M. 1975. 'Classification of Suicidal Behaviour: Quantifying Intent and Medical Lethality'. *American Journal of Psychiatry 132* (1975), 285-7.

Berhardt, G.R. and Praeger, S.G. 1983. 'After Suicide: Meeting the Needs of Survivors' *American Personnel & Guidance* (1983 March) Washington D.C.

Birtchnell, J. 1973. 'The special place of psychotherapy in the treatment of attempted suicide, and the special type of psychotherapy required'.

In *What is Psychotherapy?   Proceedings of the Ninth International Congress of Psychotherapy.   Oslo*, 316-318.

Boadt, L. 1969. *Reading the Old Testament - an Introduction*. New York: Paulist Press.

Bock, E.W. and Webber, J.L. 1972. 'Suicide & the Elderly: isolating widowhood and mitigating alternatives': *Journal of Marriage and The Family 34* (1972), 24-31.

Bongar, B.M. 1992. *Suicide - Guidelines for Assessment, Management and Treatment*. Oxford: OUP.

Bonhoeffer, D. 1959. *Letters and Papers from Prison*. London: Fontana 1971, *Ethics*. E. T. London: SCM (Munich, 1949).

Bornkamm, Gunther. 1969. *Paul*. London: SCM.

Bowlby, J. and Parkes, C.H. 1970. 'Separation and Loss within the Family.' In *The Child in His Family* Vol I. Eds. E.J. Anthony and C. Kouparnik. New York: Wiley Interscience: 197-216.

Bowlby, J. 1980. *Sadness and Depression. Vol III*. New York: Basic Books.

Bowlby, J. 1985. 'Attachment and loss'. In his *Sadness and Depression Vol. III*. Harmondsworth: Penguin.

Brennan, T. and Auslander, N. 1979. *Adult Loneliness: An Exploratory Study of Social and Psychological Predisposition and Theory*. Boulder Co., Behavioural Research Institute.

Briggs, D.C. 1970. *Your Child's Self-Esteem*. New York: Doubleday Brody, B.A. *1989, Suicide & Euthanasia - historical and contemporary themes*. London.

Buber, M. 1979. *Between Man and Man*. London: Collins Fount.

130   Christopher Tadman-Robins

Buhler, C. 1969. 'Loneliness in Maturity'. *Journal of Humanistic Psychology 9* (1969), 167-181.

Bulusu, L. and Alderson, M. 1984. 'Suicides 1950-82'. *Population Census and Survey Trends 35* (1984 Spring).

Burglass, D. and Hornton, J. 1974. 'A scale for predicting subsequent suicidal behaviour'. *British Journal of Psychiatry 124* (1974), 573-8.

Burnet, J. 1892. *Early Greek Philosophy*. London.

Calhoun, L.G., Selby, J.W., Selby, L.E. 1982. 'The Psychological aftermath of suicide: Analysis of Current Evidence'. *Clinical Psychology Review 2* (1982), 409-420.

Campbell, A.V. 1981. *Rediscovering Pastoral Care*. London: Darton, Longman & Todd.

Campbell, Robert and Collinson, Diane. 1988. *Ending Lives*. Oxford: Blackwell O.U.

Camus, Albert 1955. *The Myth of Sisyphus & Other Essays*. Trans. Justin O'Brien, New York: Random House.

Carr, G. Lloyd. 1990. *After the Storm - Hope in the Wake of Suicide* Leicester: Inter-Varsity Press.

Carr, W. 1989. *The Pastor as Theologian*. London: SPCK.

Catalan, J., Edmond, G., Ennis J. 1984. 'The Effects of non-prescribing of anxiolytics in General Effects' *British Journal of Psychiatry 144* (1984), 593-602.

Clark, David & Sarah. 1993. *The Dark Uncertainty - Wrestling with Suffering and Death*. London: Darton, Longman & Todd.

Clemons, James T. 1990. *What does the Bible say about Suicide?* Minneapolis: Fortress Press.

Cobb, Richard. 1974. 'Death in Paris 1979-1801' In *The Oxford Book of Death*. Oxford: OUP.

Coleman, J. S. 1974. *Youth: Transition of Adulthood*. Chicago: University Press.

Cook, David. 1993. *Patients' Choice*. London: Hodder & Stouton.

Cumming, E. and Lazer, C. 1981. 'Kinship Structure & Suicide: a theoretical link'. *Canadian Review of Sociology and Anthropology 18.* (1981), 271-282.

Curran, D. G. 1987. *Adolescent Suicidal Behaviour*. London: Hemisphere Publications.

Dannigelis, N. and Pope, W. 1979. 'Durkhéim's Theory of Suicide as Applied to the family: An Empirical Test'. *Social Forces 57* (1979), 1081-1106.

Daube, David. 1962. 'Death as a Release in the Bible' *Novum Testament 5* (1962) 82-104.

Diekstra, R. 1996. 'The Epidemiology of Suicide and Parasuicide' *Arch. Suicide Research 2*, 1-29.

Dockar-Drysdale, B.E. 1990. *The Provision of Primary Experience in a Therapeutic School*. London: Free Association.

Dodd, C. H. 1959. *The Epistle of Paul to the Romans*. London: Fontana. 1959, *The Meaning of Paul for Today*. Glasgow: Fount.

Dodds, E. R. 1965. *Pagan & Christian in an Age of Anxiety*. Cambridge: C.U.P.

Donne, John. 1984. *Biathanatos*. Ed. E. W. Sullivan II. Delaware: University of Delaware Press.

Dooley, E. 1990. 'Prison Suicide in England and Wales 1972-1987'. *British Journal of Psychiatry 156* (1990), 40-45.

Droge, Arthur, J. and Tabor, James. D. 1992. *A Noble Death - Suicide among Christians and Jews in Antiquity.* San Fransisco: Harper Collins.

Duffy, J. C. and Kreitman, N. 1977. 'Parasuicide in Edinburgh - A Seven Year Review 1968 - 74'. *British Journal of Psychiatry 130* (1977), 534-43.

Dunne, E. J., McIntosh, J.C., Dunne-Maxim, K. 1987. *Suicide and its Aftermath - Understanding and Counselling the Survivors.* London: W.W. Norton & Co.

Durkhéim, E. 1951. *Suicide: A study in Sociology.* Glencoe L. L. Free Press.

Dyre, R. C., Goulding, R. L., Goulding, M. E. 1973. 'No Suicide Decision: Patient Monitoring of Suicide Risk'. *American Journal of Psychiatry 130.* (1973), 171-4.

Eglin, P. 1984. 'Suicide' In *Teaching Papers in Sociology.* Eds. R. J. Anderson and W. W. Sharrock. York: Longman Resources Unit.

Eldrid, John. 1988. *Caring for the Suicidal.* London: Hodder & Stoughton.

Erikson, E. H. 1965. *Childhood and Society*: London: Penguin. 1968, *Identity: Youth and Crisis.* New York: Norton Publishing.

Eskilson, A. Wiley, M. G., Buelbauer, G., Dodder, L. 1986. 'Parental Pressure, self-esteem and adolescent reported deviance'. *Adolescence 21* (1986), 501-515.

Evans, J. G. 1967. 'Deliberate Self-Poisoning in the Oxford Area.' *British Journal of Preventative and Social Medicine 21.* (1967), 97-107.

Fabry, B. 1968. *The Pursuit of Meaning.* Boston: Beacon Press.

Farberow, Norman L. 1975. *Suicide in Different Cultures.* N. York: University Park Press. 1980, *The Many Faces of Suicide: Indirect Self-destructive behaviour.* New York: McGraw-Hill.

Fagin, L 1978. *Unemployment and Health in Families* London: Department of Health and Social Security.

Farrow, S. C. 1983. 'Monitoring the Health Effects of Unemployment'. *Journal of the Royal College of Physicians 17* (1983), 99-105.

Fedden, Henry Romilly. 1938. *Suicide: A Social & Historical Study.* London: Peter Davies.

Feldman, F. 1992. *Confrontations with the Reaper* (1941) London: Penguin.

Firestone, R. W. 1997a. *'Suicide and the Inner Voice – Risk Assessment Treatment and Case Management.* London: Sage. 1997b. *'Combating Destructive Thought Processes – Voice Therapy and Separation Theory Combating Destructive Thought Processes – Voice Therapy and Separation Theory:* London: Sage. 1988. *'Voice Therapy – A psychotherapeutic Approach to Self-Destructive Behaviour.* New York: Human Sciences Press, Inc.

Forster, D. P. and Frost, C.E.B. 1985. 'Medicinal Self-poisoning and prescription frequency'. *Acta Psychiatrica Scandinavica 71* (1985), 657-74.

Foskett, J. 1984. *Meaning in Madness - The Pastor and the Mentally Ill.* London: SPCK.

Fosket, J. and Lyall, D. 1988. *Helping the Helpers - Supervision and Pastoral Care.* London: SPCK.

Fox, A. and Shewry, D. 1988. 'New Longitudinal Insights into Relationships between Unemployment and Mortality'. *Stress Medicine 4* (1988).

Freud, S. 1957. *Mourning and Melancholia* (1917) London: Hogarth Press. 1961. *The Ego and the Id* (1923) London: Hogarth Press.

1957. *Inhibition, Symptoms and Anxieties* (1926) London: Hogarth Press. 1958. *An Outline of Psychoanalysis* (1938) London: Hogarth Press.

Fromm, E. 1955. *The Sane Society*. New York: Holt, Rinehart and Winstone Publications.

Gaer, D. M. 1976. *Psychology of Loneliness*. Chicago: Adams Press.

Gelder, M, Gath, D., and Mayou, R. 1989. *Oxford Textbook of Psychiatry* (2nd edition), Oxford: OUP.

Gibbs, J. P. and Martin, W. T. 1964. *Status Integration and Suicide: A Sociological Study*. Eugene: University of Oregon Books.

Giddens, Anthony. 1971. *The Sociology of Suicide* (1965) London: Hodder & Stouton.

Ginsberg, G. P. 1971. 'Public Conceptions and Attitudes about Suicide.' *Journal of Health and Social Behaviour 12* (1971), 200-7.

Glover, Jonathan. 1990. *Causing Death and Saving Lives*. London: Penguin.

Green, Gerard. 1992. *Coping with Suicide*. Dublin: Columbia Press.

Green, Laurie. 1990. *Let's Do Theology*. London: Mowbray.

Gupta, K., Sivakumar, K. and Smeeton, N. 1995. 'Deliberate self-harm: A comparison of first-time cases and cases with a prior history' *Irish Journal of Psychological Medicine, 12,4,*, 131-134.

Gurland, B. J. and Cross, P.S. 1983. 'Suicide among the Elderly'. In *The Acting out Elderly*. Eds. M. K. Aronson, R. Bennets and B. J. Gurland. New York: Haworth: 55-65.

Gustafson, James. 1984. *Ethics and Theology*. Chicago: University Press.

Gutierrez, P., King, C.A. and Ghaziuddin, N. 1996. 'Adolescent attitudes about death in relation to suicidality' *Suicide and Life – Threatening Behaviour 26,1.* 8-18.

Hafen, B. Q. and Frandsen, K. J. 1986. *Youth Suicide: Depression and Loneliness.* Evergreen, Colorado: Cordillera Press.

Halburachs, Maurice. 1978. *The Causes of Suicide.* E. T. London: Routledge and Kegan Paul.

Hanflung, Oswald. 1987. *Life and Meaning.* Oxford: Blackwell O.U.

Harris, J. Rendel. 1900. 'Did Judas Really Commit Suicide'. *American Journal of Theology 4.* (1900, 490-513).

Hauser, M. J. 1983. 'Bereavement for Widows'. *Journal of Psychosocial Nursing and Mental Health Services 21 (9)* (1983), 22-31.

Hauser, M. J. 1983. 'Special Aspects of Grief after Suicide'. In *The Aftermath of Suicide, understanding and Counselling the Survivors.* Eds. K. Dunne-Martin, E. J. Dunne and J. McIntosh. New York: W. W. Norton.

Hawton, K. 1994. 'Causes and Opportunities for Prevention' in *The Prevention of Suicide,* Eds. R. Jenkins, S. Griffiths, I. Wylie, et. al. London: HMSO. 1986. *Suicide and Attempted Suicide among children and Adolescents.* Beverley Hills; Sage. 1987. 'Assessment of Suicide Risk'. *British Journal of Psychiatry 150* (1987).

Hawton, K. and Bladstock, E. 1976. 'General Practice Aspects of Self-Poisoning and Self-Injury'. *Psychological Medicine 6* (1976), 571-5.

Hawton, K. and Catalan, J. 1982. *Attempted Suicide: Practical Guide to its Nature and Management.* Oxford: OUP.

Hawton, K., Fagg, J. and McKeown. 1989. 'Alcoholism, Alcohol and Attempted Suicide'. *Alcohol and Alcoholism 24.*

Hawton, K., Fagg, J. and Hawkins, M. 1993. 'Factors Associated with Suicide after Parasuicide in Young People'. *British Medical Journal* 306, 1641-1644.

Hawton, K., O'Grady., J, Osborn, M. and Cole, D. 1982. 'Adolescents who take Overdoses'. *British Journal of Psychiatry 140* (1982), 118-23.

Hawton, K. and Rose, J. 1986. 'Unemployment and Attempted Suicide among men in Oxford'. *Health Trends* (1986).

Heikkinen, M., Isometsa, E., Marttunen, M., Aro, H. and Lonnqvist, J. 1995. 'Social Factors in Suicide' *British Journal of Psychiatry 167*, 747-753.

Hill, K. 1995. *The Long Sleep – Young People and Suicide* London: Virago Press Department of Health. 1992. *The Health of the Nation - A Strategy for Health in England.* London: HMSO. 1993. *The Health of the Nation - One Year On.* London; HMSO.

Heasman, K. 1969. *An Introduction to Pastoral Counselling.* London: Constable.

Hendin. 1987. 'Youth Suicide: A Psychological Perspective.' *Suicide and Life-Threatening Behaviour 17* (1987), 151-165.

Henry, A.F. and Short, J.F. 1954. *Suicide and Homicide.* New York: Free Press.

Hillman, James. 1965. *Suicide and the Soul.* Dallas, Texas: Spring Publications.

Holden, C. 1986. 'Youth Suicide: New Research focuses on a Growing Social Problem'. *Science, 233* (1986), 839-841.

Holland, R. F. 1969. 'Suicide'. In *Talk of God.* Ed. G. Vesey. London: Macmillan.

Home Office. 1984. *Suicides in Prison - Report by H. M. Chief Inspector of Prisons.* London: HMSO.

Howard League for Penal Reform. 1989. *Suicides at Leeds Prison: An Enquiry into the Deaths of Five Teenagers during 1988/89.* London: HMSO. 1992. *Suicides in Feltham* London: HMSO. 1993. *Dying Inside - Suicides in Prison.* London: HMSO.

Hume, David. 1975. *Dialogues Concerning Natural Religion.* New York: Hafner Publishing.

Israel, Martin. 1983. *The Spirit of Counsel.* Oxford: Mowbray. 1984. *Healing as Sacrament.* London: Darton, Longmann and Todd.

Kane, T. C. 1967. 'Suicide'. In *The New Catholic Encyclopaedia.* Vol. XIII Ed. McGraw-Hill. N. York: 1967: 781-783.

Kant, I. 1948. *Groundworks of the Metaphysics of Morals.* E.T. H. J. Paton. London.

Kaplan, H.I. and Sadock, B.J. 1985. *Comprehensive Textbook of Psychiatry.* Rev. Edn. London: Williams & Wilkins.

Kast, V. 1988. *A Time to Mourn - growing through the Grief Process.* E. T. Einsiedlm, Switzerland: Diamon Verlag.

Kerfoot, M., Dyer, E., Harrington, V., Woodham, A. and Harrington, R. 1996. 'Correlates and short-term course of self-poisoning in adolescents' *British Journal of Psychiatry 168,* 1, 38-42.

Kienhorst, I. W. M., DeWilde, E. J. and Diekstra, R. F. W. 1995. Suicidal Behaviour in Adolescents' *Arch. Suicide Research 1,* 185-209.

Kienhorst, I. W. M., DeWilde, E. J., Diekstra, R. and Wolters, W. 1995. 'Adolescents' image of their suicide attempt' *Journal of the American Academy of Child and Adolescent Psychiatry* 34, 5, 623-628.

Kier, Norman. 1986. *I Can't face Tomorrow - Help for those troubled by thoughts of Suicide.* Wellingborough: Thompson Publishing.

Kirschenbaum, H. and Henderson, V.L. 1989. *The Carl Rogers Reader*. London: Constable.

Klerman, H. 1986. *Suicide and Depression Among Adolescents and Young Adults*. Washington, D. C. American Psychiatric Press Inc.

Koocher, P. G. 1974. 'Talking with Children about Death'. *American Journal of Orthopsychiatry 44* (1974), 404-411.

Koopmans, M. 1995. 'A case of family dysfunction and teenage suicide attempt: Applicability of a family systems paradigm'. *Adolescence*, 30, 117 87-94.

Kreitman, N. and Philip, A.E. 1969. *'Parasuicide' British Journal of Psychiatry 115* (1969), 746-7.

Kreitman, N, and Chowdhury, N. 1973. *'Distress Behaviour - A Study of Selected Samaritan Clients and Parasuicides'. British Journal of Psychiatry 123* (1973), 1-8.

Kreitman, N., Carstairs, V. and Duffy, J. 1991. 'Association of Age and Social Class with Suicide among men in Great Britain'. *Journal of Epidemiology and Community Health 45* (1991), 195-202.

Kübler-Ross, Elisabeth. 1973. *On Death and Dying*. London: Tavistock & Routledge.

Kuitert, Harry. 1985. 'Have Christians the Right to Kill Themselves? From Self-Murder to Self Killing' In *Suicide and the Right to Die*. Eds. Jacques Pohier and Dictman Hieth. Edinburgh: T. & T. Clark: 100-106.

Kutash, I. L. and Wolf, A. 1986. *Psychotherapist's Casebook*. London: Jossey-Bass Publishers.

Lake, Frank. 1966. *Clinical Theology - The Theological and Psychiatric Basis to Clinical Pastoral Care*. London: Darton, Longman & Todd.

Lake, Tony. 1944. *Living with Grief - Bereavement Through Suicide.* London: Sheldon Press.

Leenaars, A.J. and Wenkstern, S. 1991. *Suicide Prevention in School.* London: Hemisphere Publishing.

Lefébure, M. and Schauder, H. 1982. *Conversations on Counselling.* Edinburgh: T & T. Clark.

Lehrman, S. R. 1973. 'Reactions to Untimely Death'. In *The Interpretation of Death.* Ed. H. M. Ruiteenbeek. New York: Jason Aronson: 222-236.

Leonardson, G. R. 1986. 'The Relationship between Self-Concept and Selected Academic and Personal Factors'. *Adolescence 21* (1986), 467-474.

Liebling, Alison. 1992. *Suicide in Prison* - London: Routledge. 1993. 'Suicide and Suicide Attempts in Prison'. *Prison Service Chaplaincy Review 10* (1993), 76-79.

Liebling, A. and Krarup, H. 1993. 'Suicide Attempts and Self-injury in Male Prisons'. *Home Office Research and Planning Unit Report* (1993, September).

Lightfoot, J. B. 1893. *The Apostolic Fathers: Revised Texts with Short Introductions and E.T.* London: Macmillan.

Litman, R. E. 1970. 'Management of Suicidal Patients in Private Practice'. In *The Psychology of Suicide.* Eds. E. S. Schneidman, N. L. Farberow, R. E. Litman. New York: Science House.

Long, V.O. 1987. 'The Pursuit of Happiness: Feeling Good about Yourself, problems and prescription'. *Counselling Interview 19* (1987), 15-17.

Maltsberger, John T. 1986. *Suicide Risk - The Formulation of Clinical Judgement.* New York: University Press.

Martin, G., Rozanes, P., Pearce, C. and Allison, S. 1995. Adolescent suicide, depression and family dysfunction' *Acta Psychiatrica Scandinavica* 92. 5, 336-344.

Martunnen, M. J., Aro, H. M. and Lonnqvist, J. K. 1993. 'Adolescence and suicide in a review of psychological autopsy studies' *European Child and Adolescent Psychiary, 2,* 10-18.

Maslow, A. H. 1964. *Religious Values and Peak Experiences.* London: Viking Press.

Maslow, A. H. 1973. The Further Reaches of Human Nature. London: Penguin.

May, R. 1953. *Man's Search for Himself.* New York: Delta Books.

Mearns, D. and Thorne, B. 1988. *Person-Centred Counselling in Action.* London: Sage Publications.

Mearns, D. and Dryden, W. 1990. *Experience of Counselling in Action.* London: Sage Publications.

Melinsky, M. A. H. 1970. *Religion and Medicine.* London: SCM.

Meyaroff, M. 1971. *On Caring.* New York: Harper Row.

Minkoff, K. 1973. 'Hopelessness, Depression & Attempted Suicide'. *American Journal of Psychiatry 130* (1973), 455-459.

Mitchell, Basil. 1971. *The Philosophy of Religion.* Oxford: OUP.

Moltmann, Jürgen. 1974. *The Crucified God.* London: SCM.

Morgan, H. G. 1979. *Death Wishes* Chichester: John Wiley & Sons Ltd.

Morgan, H. G., Barton, J., Pottle, S., Pocock, H., Burns-Cox, C. J. 1975. 'Deliberate Self-Harm: A follow-up of 279 Patents'. *British Journal of Psychiatry 126.* 564-74; *128*: 361-8.

Monahan, W. B. 1927. *The Moral Theology of St. Thomas Aquinas.* Worcester: Trinity Press.

Montgomary, S.A. 1991. *Suicide and Attempted Suicide - Risk Factors and Management.* London.

Mrazec, P., Lynch, M. and Bentovim, A. 1983. 'Sexual Abuse of Children in the United Kingdom' *Child Abuse and Neglect, 7* 147-153.

Mussaph-Andriessi, R. C. 1981. *From Torah to Kabbalah.* London: SCM.

McCaughey, J. David. 1967. 'Suicide (Some Theological Considerations)' *Theology 70* (1967) 63-68.

McClure, G. M. G. 1981. 'Trends in Suicide Rate for England and Wales 1975-1980'. *British Journal of Psychiatry 144* (1981), 119-126.

McCullock, J. W. and Philip, A. E. 1972. *Suicidal Behaviour.* Oxford: Pergamon.

McDonald, H. and Murphy, T. 1990. *Sleepless Souls - Suicide in Early Modern England* Oxford: Clarendon Press.

McGee, J. 1972. *Survivors of Suicide* Illinois: Charles C. Thomas.

McIntosh, John L. 1985. *Research on Suicide (A Bibliography).* London.

McIntyre, A, Angle, C. and Stryppler, L. 1972. 'The Concept of Death in mid-western Children and Youth'. *American Journal of Diseases of Children 123.* (1972), 527-532.

Nietzsche, F. 1958. *Thus Spake Zarathustra.* London: Dent and Dutton.

Nock, A. D. 1933. *Conversion: The Old and The New in Religion from Alexander the Great to Augustine of Hippo.* Oxford: Clarendon Press.

Oddie, William. 1989. *The Crockford's File - Gareth Bennett and the Death of the Anglican Mind.* London: Hamish Hamilton.

Osgood, N. J. and McIntosh, J. L.   1986.   *Suicide and The Elderly.* Westport, C. T: Greenwood Press.

O'Shea, Brian. 1989. *Essays in Psychiatry.* London.

Orbach, I. and Glauman, H. 1979. 'Children's Perception of Death as a defensive Process'. *Journal of Psychology 88* (1979), 671-674.

Parkes, C. M.   1986.   *Bereavement: Studies of Grief in Adult Life.* Harmondsworth: Penguin.

Pattison, S. 1988. *A Critique of Pastoral Care.* London: SCM.

Payical, E. S, Prusoff, B.A, and Myers, J. K. 1975. Suicide Attempts and Recent Live Events: A Controlled Comparison'. *Archives of General Psychiatry 32* (1975), 327-33.

Peplan, L. A. and Perlman, D. 1982. 'Perspectives on Loneliness'. In *A Sourcebook of Current Theory, Research and Therapy.* Eds. L. A. Peplan and D. Perlman. New York: John Wiley and Sons.

Perlin, S. 1975. *A Handbook for the Study of Suicide.* Oxford: OUP.

Perry, C. 1991. *Listen to the Voice Within - A Jungian Approach to Pastoral Care.* London: SPCK.

Pfeffer, C. R. 1989. *Suicide among Youth - risk prevention.* New York: John Wiley and Sons.

Platt, S. and Kreitman, N. 1984(a). 'Trends in Parasuicide and unemployment among men in Edinburgh 1968-82'. *British Medical Journal* (1984, October), 1029-1032. 1984(b). 'Is Unemployment a Cause of Parasuicide?'. *British Medical Journal 290* (1984), 161.

Pliny. 1924. *Letters.* E. T. W. Melmouth and W. M. L.Hutchingson. Cambridge Mass: Harvard Press.

Pohier, J. and Mieth, D. 1985. *Suicide and the Right to Die.* E. T. Edinburgh: T & T Clark.

Population Censuses and Surveys. 1993. *Mortality Statistics - Review of the Registrar General on Deaths in England and Wales 1991.* Series DH1 No. 26. 1993. Deaths from injury and poisoning: External Causes - 1992 registrations. OPCS Monior (1993, July).

Population Censuses and Surveys. 1993. *Suicide Deaths in England and Wales: Trends in factors associated with suicide deaths.* No. 69 and 71 (1993, Spring).

Prison Service. 1990. *Suicide and Self-harm in Prison Service Establishments.* Report by H.M. Chief Inspector of Prisons: HMSO.

Prison Service. 1992. *Caring for Prisoners at Risk of Suicide and Self-injury - The Way Forward.* Suicide Awareness Support Unit. 1992. Report on Swansea Prison's Listener Scheme'. In *Prison Report - The Prison Reform Trust.* Ed. Brian Davies. 1993. 'New Deal for the Desperate'. In *Prison Report - The Prison Reform Trust.* Ed. Adam Sampson. 1993. *Suicide and Self-harm in Prison Service Establishments.* Report of a Review by HM Chief Inspector of Prisons: HMSO. 1983. *Arrangements for the Prevention of Suicide in Prisons.* Prison Reform Trust Submission (1983, June).

Pritchard, C. 1995. *Suicide – The Ultimate Rejection- A Psycho-social Study.* Buckingham: Open University Press.

Raphael, B. 1985. *The Anatomy of Bereavement, A Handbook for the Caring Professions.* London: Hutchinson.

Reiss, D. 1981. *The Family's Construction of Reality.* Cambridge, Mass: Harvard University Press.

Resnick, H. L. P. 1972. 'Psychological Resynthsis: A clinical approach to the survivors of death by suicide'. In *Survivors of Suicide,* Ed. A. C. Cain, Springfield Illinois.

Roberts, J. and Hawton, K. 1980. 'Child Abuse and Attempted Suicide' *British Journal of Psychiatry 137* (1980) 319-23.

Rogers, Carl R.   1967.   *A Therapist's View of Psychotherapy: On Becoming a Person.* London: Constable and Co.   1980.   *A Way of Being.* Boston: Houghton Mifflin Co.

Rogers, J., Sheldon, A., Barwick, C., Letofsky, K. and Lanch, B.   1982. 'Help for Families of Suicide: Survivors Support Programme'. *American Journal of Psychiatry.* (1982), 444-449.

Roetzel, Calvin J.   1975.   *The Letters of Paul - Conversations in Context* London: SCM.

Rosenthal, N.   1983.   'Death Education and Suicide Potentiality'. *Death Education 7* (1983, 39-51).

Rowe, D.   1979.   *The Courage to Live.* London: Routledge and Kegan Paul.   1984.   *Depression - The Way out of Your Prison.* London: Routledge and Kegan Paul.

Rowley, H. H.   1956.   *The Faith of Israel.* London; SCM.

Royal College of General Practitioners.   1981.   'Prevention of Psychiatric Disorders in General Practice'. *General Practice 20* (1981) 8-12.

Rubey, C. T.and Clarke, D. C.   1987.   'Suicide Survivors and the Clergy'. In *The Aftermath of Suicide.*   Eds. E. J. Dunne, J. McIntosh and K. Dunne-Martin. New York: W. W. Norton.

Rudestan, K. E.   1977.   'Physical and Psychological responses to Suicide in the Family. *Journal of Consulting and Clinical Psychology 45* (1977), 162-170.

Rudestan, K. E. and Imbroll, D.   1983.   'Societal Reaction to a child's death by suicide'. *Journal of Consulting and Clinical Psychology 51* (1983) 461-462.

Runeson, B., Eklund, G. and Wasserman, D.   1996.   'Living Conditions of Suicide attempters: a case control study'   *Acta Psychiatrica Scandinavica 94,* 125-132.

Sainsbury, Peter. 1955. *Suicide in London: An Ecological Study.* London: Chapman and Hall.

Samaritans. 1984. *Answers to Suicide.* London: Constable. 1990-94. *Samaritan News.* Issues 15-24. 1992. *Reach Out .... We'll be there.* (Samaritan Outreach Programme) Slough: The Samaritans. 1993. *Every Two Hours - Understanding Suicide.* (Annual Report 1992-1993) Slough: The Samaritans. 1996. *Challenging the Taboo – Attitudes towards suicide and depression.* 1997a. *Hope at the End of a Line – Annual Review.* 1997b. *Exploring the Taboo – Attitudes of Young People Towards Suicide and Depression.*

Schneidman, E. S. 1974. *Voices of Death: Personal Documents from People Facing Death.* New York: Bantam Books. 1985. *Definitions of Suicide* New York: John Wiley and Son. 1976. *Suicidology: Contemporary Developments.* New York: Grune and Stratton.

Scott, Donald. 1989. *Coping with Suicide.* London: Sheldon Press.

Scottish Council for Civil Liberties. 1987. *Facing Reality - The Scottish Prison Crisis in the 1980's.*

Shreeve, Caroline. 1984. *Depression - its causes and How to Overcome it.* Wellinborough: Thurston Press.

Shulman K. 1978. 'Suicide and Parasuicide in Old Age: A Review'. *Age and Ageing 7* (1978), 201-209.

Shutt, R. J. H. 1978. *Studies in Josephus.* London: SPCK.

Singer, Peter. 1986. *Applied Ethics.* Oxford: OUP.

Smith, J. 1986. *Coping with Suicide.* New York: Rosen Publishing.

Social Responsibility , Church Assembly Board Of. 1959. *Ought Suicide to be a Crime?* Westminster: Church House.

Social Responsibility, Church of Scotland General Assembly. 1977. *Euthanasia - Theological Considerations.* Edinburgh: Committee of Church and Nation. 1991. *Euthanasia.* Edinburgh: Board of Social

Responsibility. 1994. *Suicide: The Taking of One's Life*. Report to the General Assembly.

Social Responsibility, The Methodist Church. 1961. *Methodist Conference Minutes*. London: Department of Christian Citizenship.

Social Responsibility, The Roman Catholic Church. *Les Dix Commandments - Le Suicide*. Catholic Bishops' Conference of England and Wales.

Most Reverend Dermot Clifford, Archbishop of Cashel and Emly. *Suicide - A Permanent Solution to a temporary problem?* Dublin: Veritas.

Stack, S. 1982. 'Suicide: a decade review of the sociological literature? *Deviant Behaviour 4*. (1982), 41-66.

Stanway, A. 1981. *Overcoming Depression* Feltham: Hamlyn.

Stenager, E. and Jenson, K. 1994. 'Attempted Suicide and Contact with the Primary Health Authorities. '.*Acta Psychiatrica Scandinavica 90, 109-113*.

Stengel, E. 1964. *Suicide and Attempted Suicide*. Middlesex: Pelican.

St. John-Stevas, Norman. 1961. *Life, Death and The Law*. London: Eyre and Spottiswoode.

Stillion, J. H. McDowell, E.E., May, J. H. 1989. *Suicide Across the Life Span - Premature Exits*. New York: Hemisphere Publishing Corporation.

Stroebe, M.S.and Strobe, W. 1983. 'Who Suffers More? Sex differences in health risks of the widowed? *Psychological Bulletin 9*. (1983), 279-301.

Suominen, K., Henriksson, M., Suokas, J., Isometsa, E., Ostamo, A., and Lonnqvist, J. 1996. 'Mental Disorders and Comorbidity in Attempted Suicide' *Scandinavica Acta Psychiatrica* 94, 234-240.

Sym, John. 1988. *Life Preservation against Self-killing*. London: Penguin.

Thompson, Ian E. 1976. 'Suicide: Its Challenge to Philosophy'. *Contact 54* (1976) 3.

Thorne, B. 1991 (a). *Behold the Man - A Therapist's Meditations on the Passion of Jesus Christ.* London: Darton, Longmann and Todd. 1991 (b). *Person-centred Counselling, Therapeutic and Spiritual Dimensions.* London: Whurr Publishers. 1992. *Carl Rogers.* London: Sage.

Thorne, B. and Dryden, W. 1993. *Counselling: Interdisciplinary Perspectives.* Milton Keynes: Open University Press.

Tillick, Paul. 1952. *The Courage to be.* Yale: University Press.

Topp, D. 1979. 'Suicide in Prison' *British Journal of Psychiatry* 134, 24-27.

Toynbee, A. 1976. *Man's Concern with Death.* New York: McGraw-Hill.

Trenchard, L. and Warren, H. 1984. *Something to Tell You.* London: London Gay Teenage Group.

Trovato, F. 1986. 'The Relationship between marital dissolution and suicide'. *Journal of Marriage and the Family 48. (1986)*, 341-348.

Tuckman, T. and Youngman, W. F. 1968   'A Scale for Assessing Suicide Risk or Attempted Suicide'. *Journal of Clinical Psychiatry 24.* (1968), 17-19.

Vanstone, W.H. 1982. *The Stature of Waiting.* London: Darton, Longman and Todd.

Varah, Chad. 1987. *The Samaritans - Befriending the Suicidal.* Rev. Ed. London: Constable.

Vaughan, P. J. 1985. *Suicide Prevention.* Birmingham: Pepar Publications.

148   Christopher Tadman-Robins

Waldron, I. and Eyer, J. 1975. 'Socio-economic Causes of Recent Rise in death rates for 15-24 year olds'. *Social Science and Medicine 9* (1975), 383-396.

Wallance, S. E. 1977. 'On the A typicality of Suicide Bereavement'. In *Suicide and Bereavement*. Eds. B. L. Danto and H. H. Kutscher. New York: Mss Information Corps.

Wechsler, J. A. 1972. *In a Darkness*. New York: W. W. Norton Co.

Weissmann, M. M. 1974. 'The Epidemiology of Suicidal Attempts'. *Archives General Psychiatry 30*. (1974), 737-46.

Weissmann, M. M. and Klerman, G. L. 1977   'Sex differences in the epidemiology of depression'. *Archives of General Psychiatry,* 34, 98-111.

Wells, N. 1981. *Suicide and Deliberate Self-Harm*. London: Office of Health Economics. No. 69wx.

Wenz, F. V. 1981. 'Family Size, depression and parent suicide risk?' In *Depression and Suicide: medical, psychological and socio-cultural Aspects*. New York: Pergamon Press (1981), 310-315.

Wertheimer, Alison. 1991. *A Special Scar - The Experience of People Bereaved by Suicide*. London: Tavistock Routledge.

Wetzel, R. D. 1976. 'Hopelessness, Depression and Suicide Intent'. *Archives General Psychiatry 33* (1976).

White, John. 1982. *The Masks of Melancholy - A Christian Psychiatrist looks at depression and suicide*. Leicester: Inter-Varsity Press.

Whiteley, D. E. H. 1974. *The Theology of St. Paul*. Oxford: Blackwell.

Wilson, Peter. 1993. 'Suicide and Young People' *Young Minds 16* (1993).

Wittgenstein, L. 1961. *Notebooks 1914-16* Oxford: Anscombe Rhees and Von Wright.

Woolf, Lord Justice. 1990. *Prison Disturbances.* London: HMSO.

Worden, W. J. 1983. *Grief Counselling and Grief Therapy* London: Tavistock.

World Health Organisation. 1968. *Prevention of Suicide.* Geneva: WHO.

Wright, F. 1982. *Pastoral Care for Lay People.* London: SCM.

Yalom, I. D. 1980. *Existential Psychotherapy.* New York: Basic Books.

Yung, C. G.

Young, D. 1994. 'Behaviors and attributions – Family views of adolescent psychopathology' *Journal of Adolescent Research 9, 4* 427-441.

Yung, C. G. 1961. *Modern Man in Search of a Soul.* London: Routledge and Kegan Paul.

ABOUT THE AUTHOR

Christopher Tadman - Robins is a Non-Stipendiary Minister, a free-lance musician by occupation and a priest in the Church of England. He currently works as a Team Minister in the United Benefice of Shipton-u-Wychwood in rural Oxfordshire.

He is also a founder member of SASH (Suicide and Self Harm) the Oxford Diocese Working Group that is dedicated to providing a human resource for both clergy and laity who are unfamiliar with the physical and pastoral problems of self harm. For many years he served as a Magistrate and has worked in both hospital and school chaplaincies.

His education background includes a graduate degree from the prestigious Royal Northern College of Music (Manchester) Teaching and Performance Diplomas from both the Royal Academy and Royal Colleges of Music, together with a Post-Graduate Diploma in education from the Institute of Education, London University. For many years he both played as a solo pianist and was Musical Director and Principal Conductor of Northern Ballet Theatre.

His ordination training was undertaken with the Oxford Ministry Course (S. Stephen's Theological College, Oxford) where he gained a BA Hons in Theology, a Diploma in Applied Theology and a M.Th from Westminster College also a Post-Graduate Diploma in Theology and Biblical Studies from the University Continuing Education Department. Having gained in 1998 the D.Min in Theological Studies he has recently completed the requirements for the Ph.D from the Graduate Theological Foundation.